THE
COMMONSENSE
COOKERY BOOK

THE
COMMONSENSE
COOKERY BOOK

ANGUS
& ROBERTSON
PUBLISHERS

Photography by Ian Morgan

All measurements in this book conform to the Metric Cup and Spoon Measurements of the Standards Association of Australia.

ANGUS & ROBERTSON PUBLISHERS

Unit 4, Eden Park, 31 Waterloo Road,
North Ryde, NSW, Australia 2113, and
16 Golden Square, London W1R 4BN,
United Kingdom

Revised edition first published in Australia
by Angus & Robertson Publishers in 1970
Reprinted 1971, 1972, 1973
Metric edition 1974
Reprinted 1975
This full colour edition 1976
Reprinted 1986

ISBN 0 207 13328 X

Printed in Singapore

CONTENTS

KITCHEN REQUISITES ix

METRIC CUP AND SPOON MEASUREMENTS x

METRIC CONVERSIONS xii

MEAT COOKERY xiv

TERMS USED IN COOKERY xix

BREAKFAST COOKERY 1

STOCKS AND SOUPS 6

FISH 10

MEAT AND POULTRY DISHES 17

VEGETABLES 36

SALADS AND SALAD DRESSINGS 43

COLD MEAT COOKERY 47

SAVOURY DISHES 51

MILK PUDDINGS 66

STEAMED OR BOILED PUDDINGS 72

SUMMER PUDDINGS 78

FRUITS—STEWED AND CASSEROLED 85

BATTERS 88

PASTRY 90

SWEET PASTRY 95

CAKES 101

ICINGS AND FILLINGS FOR CAKES 115

BISCUITS AND SLICES 119

SCONE AND LOAF MIXTURES 128

BREADS AND YEAST COOKERY   133

SANDWICHES   138

SAUCES AND GRAVY   140

CHUTNEY, PICKLES, AND BOTTLED SAUCE   146

JAMS AND JELLIES   149

SWEETS AND CONFECTIONERY   152

DISHES SUITABLE FOR CONVALESCENTS, THE AGED AND
CHILDREN   155

MISCELLANEOUS   164

INDEX   167

ILLUSTRATIONS

Between Pages

MINESTRONE SOUP	12–13
BAKED FISH	12–13
SCALLOPED OYSTERS	28–29
BONED, STUFFED FOREQUARTER OF LAMB	28–29
CORNED BEEF	28–29
CHICKEN PIE	28–29
CRUMBED FRIED CUTLETS	44–45
GOULASH	44–45
STEAK AND KIDNEY PIE	60–61
CHEESE AND VEGETABLE BAKE	60–61
CHICKEN CASSEROLE	60–61
EGG AND BACON PIE	76–77
STEWED PEARS, STEWED RHUBARB	76–77
STRAWBERRY PANCAKES	92–93
CHRISTMAS CAKE	92–93
GINGERBREAD, MERINGUES AND SWISS ROLL	108–109
ASSORTED BISCUITS, SHORTBREAD	108–109
SCONES, DATE LOAF, PUMPKIN SCONES	140–141
BROWN BREAD, WHITE BREAD, YEAST BUNS	140–141
CHUTNEYS, PICKLES AND JAMS	140–141

KITCHEN REQUISITES

A good stove
Saucepans of various sizes
Double saucepan
Boiler and steamer
Pressure cooker
Baking dish and trivet
Frying pan
Frying basket
Omelet pan
Griller or gridiron
Ovenproof dishes
Moulds
Pudding basins
Mixing bowls
Cake tins
Sandwich tins (pair)
Swiss roll tin
Set of scales
Set of measures
Set of skewers
Set of cutters
  (pastry and biscuit)
Strainers

Flour scoop
Flour dredge
Wooden spoon
Basting spoon
Cook's knife
Vegetable knife
Kitchen fork
Corkscrew
Tin-opener
Pair of scissors
Asbestos mats
Oven holder
Clock
Storage jars
Cake cooler
Sifter
Pastry board
Rolling pin
Pastry brush
Grater
Egg whisk
Fish slice
Potato masher

METRIC CUP AND SPOON
MEASUREMENTS

All measurements in this book conform to the metric cup and spoon measurements of the Standards Association of Australia:

1 metric cup	250 ml.
1 tablespoon	20 ml.
1 teaspoon	5 ml.

Spoon measures are *level* spoonfuls.

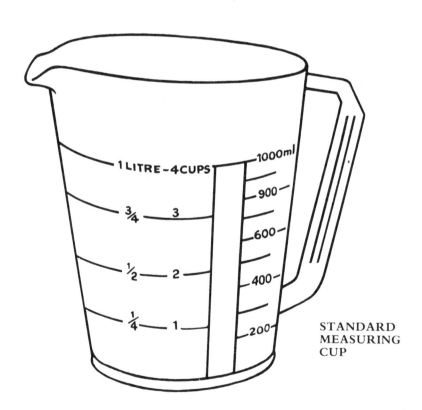

STANDARD
MEASURING
CUP

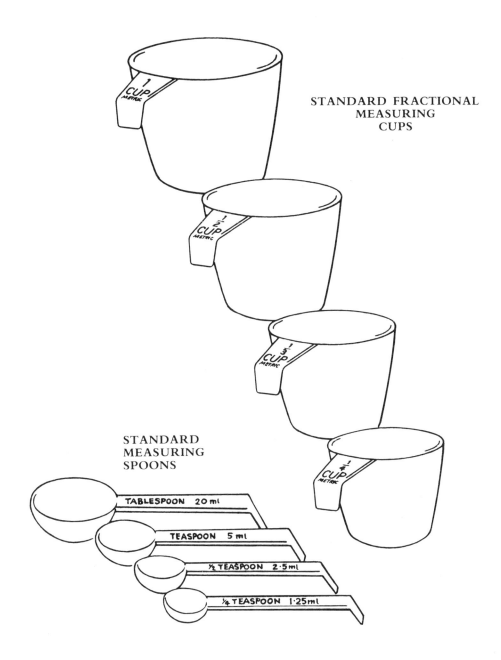

STANDARD FRACTIONAL
MEASURING
CUPS

STANDARD
MEASURING
SPOONS

TABLESPOON 20 ml

TEASPOON 5 ml

½ TEASPOON 2·5 ml

¼ TEASPOON 1·25 ml

METRIC CONVERSIONS

LENGTH MEASUREMENTS

inches	mm	cm
$\frac{1}{16}$	2	
$\frac{1}{8}$	3	
$\frac{1}{4}$	5	
$\frac{1}{2}$	10	1
$\frac{3}{4}$	20	2
1	25	2.5
2	50	5
$2\frac{1}{2}$	62	6
3		8
4		10
6		15
7		18
8		20
9		23
10		25
12		30
14		35
16		40
18		45
20		50

TEMPERATURES

100 degrees Celsius (boiling point) = 212 degrees Fahrenheit

0 degrees Celsius (freezing point) = 32 degrees Fahrenheit

Celsius (C.) into Fahrenheit (F.)

deg. C.	deg. F.	deg. C.	deg. F.
120	248	200	392
130	266	210	410
140	284	220	428
150	302	230	446
160	320	240	464
170	338	250	482
180	356	260	500
190	374		

Fahrenheit into Celsius

deg. F.	deg. C.	deg. F.	deg. C.
250	121	400	205
275	135	425	219
300	149	450	233
325	163	475	246
350	177	500	260
375	191		

For oven temperatures degrees Celsius approximately equals half of degrees Fahrenheit.

	warm		moderate			hot		very hot	
°C	150	160	180	190	200	220	230	250	260
°F	300	325	350	375	400	425	450	475	500

MEAT COOKERY

JOINTS AND THEIR ACCOMPANIMENTS

Roast beef. Yorkshire pudding; horse-radish sauce; thin brown gravy; baked vegetables.

Salted or corned beef. Carrots; turnips; suet dumplings.

Simmered mutton. Carrots; turnips; caper, onion, or parsley sauce.

Roast mutton. Baked vegetables; thin brown gravy; red currant jelly.

Roast lamb. Baked vegetables; mint sauce; thin brown gravy.

Roast veal. Boiled ham or bacon; thick brown gravy; slices of lemon, forcemeat, or seasoning.

Roast pork. Sage and onion seasoning; baked vegetables; apple sauce; thick brown gravy.

TIMETABLE FOR COOKING MEATS

Beef and mutton. 50 minutes to each kg (thick joints); 40-45 minutes to each kg (thin joints).

Pork and veal. 70 minutes to each kg.

Corned round and corned brisket. 80 minutes to each kg.

Pickled pork. 80 minutes to each kg.

Ham. 80 minutes to each kg.

Tongue. 2 to 3 hours, according to size.

These times vary according to taste.

CUTS OF MEAT AND HOW TO COOK THEM

(By courtesy of the Meat and Allied Trades Federation of Australia)

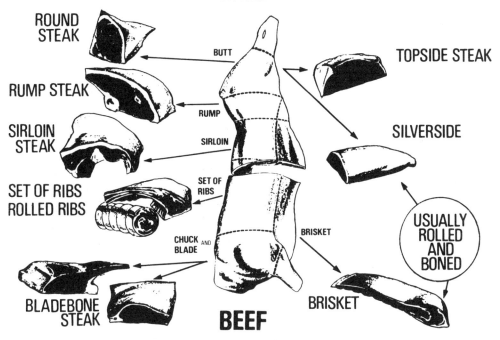

ROUND STEAK

RUMP STEAK

SIRLOIN STEAK

SET OF RIBS ROLLED RIBS

BLADEBONE STEAK

BUTT

RUMP

SIRLOIN

SET OF RIBS

CHUCK AND BLADE

BRISKET

TOPSIDE STEAK

SILVERSIDE

USUALLY ROLLED AND BONED

BRISKET

BEEF

Beef Cuts	Cooking Uses
Topside and Round ..	{ Frying and/or Braising Steak, Roast, Seasoned and Steam
Silverside (Corned) ..	Simmer
Sirloin as Joint	Roast
Sirloin, T-Bone and Porterhouse	Grill or Fry
Rump	Grill or Fry
Fillet	Grill or Fry
Leg	Brawn or Gravy Beef for Soup
Rib, Rolled or Bone in Blade and Oyster Blade	Braise, Fry or Roast
Chuck	Braise, Curry, Stew, Mince or Roast
Brisket (Corned)	Simmer
Shin	Brawn or Gravy Beef for Soup

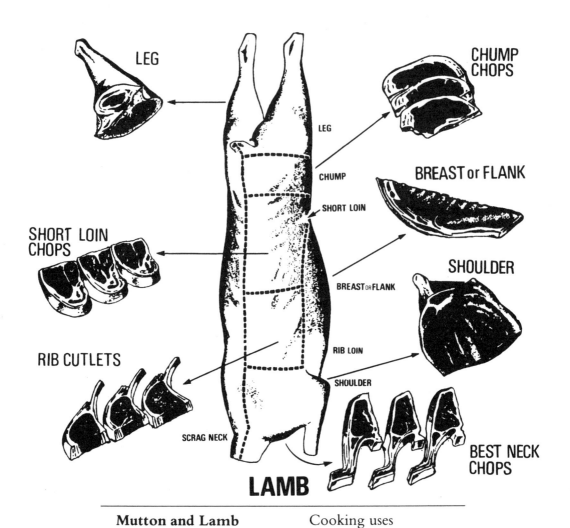

LEG

CHUMP CHOPS

BREAST or FLANK

SHORT LOIN CHOPS

SHOULDER

RIB CUTLETS

BEST NECK CHOPS

LEG

CHUMP

SHORT LOIN

BREAST or FLANK

RIB LOIN

SHOULDER

SCRAG NECK

LAMB

Mutton and Lamb	Cooking uses
Leg	Roast or Simmer
Chump or Fillet	Chump Chops—Grill or Fry Fillet—to Roast
Short Loin Chops . ..	Grill or Fry
Cutlets	Grill or Fry
Shoulder	Boned for Seasoning Boned & Rolled or on the Bone Roast Rolled and Corned Chops—Stew or Braise
Fore-quarter Chops ..	Stew or Braise
Neck and Shank	Braise, Stew, Soup
Breast	Corned, Roast or Braise
Kidney	Grill, Braise, Stew

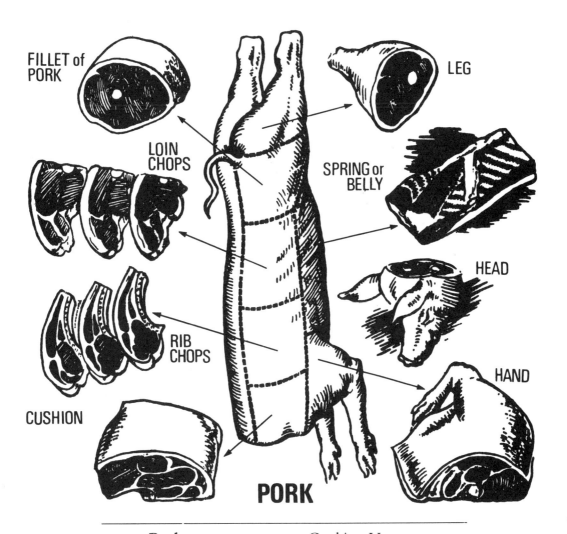

FILLET of PORK

LEG

LOIN CHOPS

SPRING or BELLY

HEAD

RIB CHOPS

HAND

CUSHION

PORK

Pork	Cooking Uses
Leg	Roast
Loin	Roast Chops to Grill or Fry
Fore-loin (Cushion) ..	Roast. Chops to Grill or Fry
Hand (Corned)	Boil and Simmer
Spring or Belly	Roast. If Corned—Simmer
Head, Pig's Cheek ..	Brawn

ROASTING AND BAKING WITH A MEAT THERMOMETER

MEAT	TEMPERATURE C	
Beef	rare	60
	medium	70
	well done	75
Lamb	medium	75
	well done	80
Mutton	well done	80
Veal	well done	75
Fresh pork	well done	85
Cured pork	well done	75
Tender ham	well done	65
Whole poultry	well done	85
Boneless poultry	well done	75

Note: These temperatures only act as a guide.

TERMS USED IN COOKERY

Au gratin. A term applied to dishes prepared with or without sauce, topped with breadcrumbs or grated cheese or both, dotted with butter and browned in the oven or under the griller.

Blanch. Plunge into boiling water briefly and drain, or cover with cold water and bring to the boil and drain.

Blend. Combine ingredients with a spoon, using a wide circular motion, and mix to a smooth paste using a cold liquid.

Boiling point. 100°C. When bubbles reach the surface of a liquid and break.

Bouquet garni. A bunch of herbs consisting of 3 sprigs of parsley, 2 sprigs of thyme, 1 sprig of marjoram and a bay leaf tied together with a piece of string and placed in a simmering sauce or stew. If dried herbs are used they should be wrapped in a piece of wet cheesecloth, then dried, for easy removal at the end of cooking time.

Caramel. Sugar cooked over moderate heat and stirred constantly until it turns into a dark brown syrup. Used as a colouring for soups, stews, gravies and sauces.

Compote. Fresh or dried fruit or vegetables cooked in syrup and served cold.

Condensed milk. Whole milk concentrated by evaporating part of the water content. It is available both sweetened and unsweetened; the unsweetened form is known as evaporated milk.

Croûtons. Small squares of bread fried in butter and served with soup.

Dice. Cut into very small cubes.

Entrée. A side or made dish such as stew, cutlets, fillets of game, ham, tongue, or salad.

Fillet. An undercut of meat; cut of meat or fish without skin or bone.

Fondant. A type of French confection; foundations for sweets.

Garnish. Ornament or decorate food.

Gâteau. A round flat cake or jelly used as a foundation for sweets.

Glaze. Brush over with liquid such as egg, milk, sugar and water, or aspic, to improve the appearance.

Knead. Blend a dough by first flattening it on a floured board and then turning the outside edge farthest from you to the centre, pressing down several times with the heels of your hands, pushing the dough away from you. The dough should then be turned a quarter of the way round, and the process repeated until the dough becomes satiny and elastic—generally after 5 to 10 minutes of energetic kneading.

Macedoine. A combination of various kinds of fresh fruits or vegetables cut into small even-shaped pieces. A macedoine of fruit is served chilled; a macedoine of vegetables is cooked and dressed with sauce and may be served hot or cold.

Mask. Cover or coat with a thick sauce, or with aspic.

Maître d' hôtel. Butter mixed with chopped parsley, lemon juice, and salt and pepper, and served with meat or fish.

Marinade. A highly seasoned liquid made of oils, herbs and vinegar in which meat or fish is soaked for some time to impart flavour and, sometimes, to tenderize.

Panada. A thick sauce used to bind meat or fish for rissoles or croquettes.

Purée. A pulp made by forcing cooked fruits or vegetables or other solid food through a strainer, or mashing them with a wooden spoon.

Sauté. Shake over heat in a little very hot butter or fat.

Salmi. A rich stew of game.

Shortening. Any animal or vegetable fat—butter, margarine, lard or dripping.

Simmering. 80° to 85°C. When small bubbles form slowly and collapse below the surface.

Sippets. Small triangular-shaped pieces of dry toast.

Stock. A liquid made by simmering together meat bones or fish trimmings with vegetables and seasonings in water.

Tepid. Two parts of cold liquid to one part of boiling.

BREAKFAST COOKERY

FRIED BACON

1. Remove the rind from the bacon rashers, and save it to flavour soups, etc.
2. Place the bacon in frying pan.
3. Cook very slowly till the fat is transparent.
4. Serve very hot.

FRIED BACON AND TOMATO

1 rasher of bacon
1 tomato
Pinch of salt
Pinch of pepper

1. Remove rind from bacon.
2. Place bacon in a cold pan without fat and fry slowly till fat is clear.
3. Lift onto a hot dish.
4. Wash and dry tomato, cut into thick slices.
5. Place into the hot fat remaining after frying the bacon, cook slowly, turn only once and avoid breaking the slices, and sprinkle with salt and pepper.
6. Serve on rasher of bacon. Garnish with sprigs of parsley.

Note. Tomato and bacon may also be grilled.

COCOA

1 cup milk or $\frac{1}{2}$ cup milk and $\frac{1}{2}$ cup water
1 teaspoon cocoa
1 teaspoon sugar (optional)

1. Heat milk or milk-and-water mixture.
2. Pour a little heated milk onto cocoa and sugar, and blend.
3. Return all to saucepan, heat slowly and simmer 1 minute.

MILK COFFEE

1 tablespoon pure coffee, or 1
    teaspoon coffee and
    chicory
$\frac{1}{2}$ cup cold water
A few grains salt
$\frac{1}{2}$ cup boiling milk

1. Put the coffee, water, and salt into a small saucepan, put the lid on, and bring slowly to simmering point.
2. Allow to stand 1 minute with lid on.
3. Strain through a fine strainer into a jug.
4. Heat the milk.
5. To serve, pour equal quantities of coffee and milk into the cup.

Note. Coffee may be made by bringing milk, coffee, and salt to boiling point.

EGGS COOKED IN SHELLS

There are three methods of lightly cooking eggs in shells:

1. Place eggs in boiling water and simmer gently 3 minutes.
2. Place eggs in cold water, bring to the simmering point, and simmer 1 minute. (Use this method for eggs taken from the refrigerator.)
3. Have saucepan of boiling water ready, place the eggs in, lift off the heat, and allow to remain 6 to 10 minutes with lid tightly on.

EGG CUTLETS

4 tablespoons sausage meat
1 teaspoon salt
2 teaspoons chopped parsley
3 hard-cooked eggs
2 tablespoons flour
1 egg, beaten
4 tablespoons breadcrumbs
Frying fat
1 cup brown sauce or brown
    gravy (see pp. 140, 141)

1. Mix the sausage meat, salt, and chopped parsley well together.
2. Remove the shells from the eggs.
3. Cover the eggs carefully with the sausage meat, keeping them in shape.
4. Dip them in the flour, brush over with beaten egg; toss in the breadcrumbs and firm them on well.
5. Fry for 5 minutes in heated fat.
6. Drain on white paper.
7. Cut in halves lengthways.
8. Serve on a hot plate accompanied by brown sauce or brown gravy.
9. Garnish with sprigs of parsley.

EGG AND ANCHOVY

1 slice bread
¼ teaspoon anchovy paste
1 teaspoon butter
1 egg
Pinch pepper and salt

1. Toast the bread and while hot spread with anchovy paste.
2. Make butter hot in a saucepan.
3. Break egg into a basin, add pepper and salt, and put into hot butter.
4. Stir until it becomes set.
5. Spread over the toast and serve immediately.

EGG AND TOMATO

1 tomato
2 teaspoons butter
Salt and pepper to taste
1 egg (hard-cooked)
Slice of dry toast

1. Wash and cut tomato up roughly.
2. Melt butter, and fry tomato 3 minutes.
3. Add salt and pepper and simmer till tomato is cooked.
4. Cut egg in quarters lengthways, place in tomato to heat.
5. Lift egg out carefully onto toast. Cover with tomato.

FRIED EGG AND BACON

1 slice bacon
1 egg

1. Remove rind from bacon; put bacon in pan and cook until crisp.
2. Lift out and place on a hot plate.
3. If not sufficient fat in pan add a little dripping and make just warm.
4. Break the egg into a saucer and remove the white speck, slide carefully into the warm fat.
5. Cook slowly, pouring spoonfuls of fat over the egg while cooking.
6. When set, lift out with an egg slice, drain well, and place on the bacon.

POACHED EGG

$\frac{1}{2}$ teaspoon salt
6 drops vinegar
1 egg
1 slice buttered toast

1. Put about 2.5 cm of water in a small frying pan or saucepan and bring to the boil.
2. Reduce temperature and add the salt and vinegar.
3. Break the egg into a saucer.
4. Drop the egg carefully into the water.
5. Allow to simmer slowly from 3 to 5 minutes, until set.
6. Lift the egg out with a spoon or slice, and drain.
7. Place carefully on the toast, and serve at once.
8. Garnish with chopped parsley.

SCRAMBLED EGG

1 teaspoon butter
1 egg
$\frac{1}{8}$ teaspoon salt
Pinch pepper
2 tablespoons milk
$\frac{1}{4}$ teaspoon chopped parsley
1 slice hot buttered toast

1. Melt butter in saucepan.
2. Beat egg well, add salt, pepper and milk; add to melted butter.
3. Stir over gentle heat until thick, do not allow to become hard.
4. Remove from stove; add chopped parsley.
5. Pile on hot toast on a hot plate.

STEAMED EGG

1 egg
Buttered toast
Salt and pepper to taste

1. Grease 2 saucers (cups may be used) with butter.
2. Break egg carefully onto one saucer.
3. Cover with the other.
4. Stand over a saucepan of gently boiling water or in a steamer.
5. Cook slowly for about 4 minutes.
6. When set, slide it on to a piece of buttered toast.
7. Sprinkle with salt and pepper.
8. Garnish with parsley.

ROLLED OATS

1 cup water
Pinch salt
1 cup rolled oats

1. Boil water and salt.
2. Sprinkle oats in, stirring all the time.
3. Stir over heat till boiling.
4. Simmer gently 10 to 20 minutes.

WHEATMEAL PORRIDGE

4 tablespoons wheatmeal
$1\frac{1}{4}$ cups water
Pinch salt

1. Moisten wheatmeal with a little of the cold water.
2. Put remainder of water on to boil; add salt.
3. Stir in the blended wheatmeal.
4. Cook slowly 10 to 15 minutes, stirring occasionally.

Note. Wheatmeal may be soaked in water overnight. Place all in saucepan and stir over heat till boiling. Simmer 10 to 15 minutes.

BOILED RICE

5 cups water
Pinch salt
$\frac{1}{2}$ cup rice

1. Put water and salt on to boil.
2. Wash rice if necessary.
3. Add to boiling water.
4. Cook quickly without lid until tender, approximately 15 minutes.
5. Strain.

TEA

Use good quality tea.

1. Have water freshly boiled.
2. Rinse teapot with boiling water.
3. Allow 2 teaspoons tea to every $2\frac{1}{2}$ cups of water or more, according to taste.
4. Pour boiling water on leaves and allow to infuse before pouring.

STOCKS AND SOUPS

STOCK FOR CLEAR SOUP

2 kg bones
2 teaspoons salt
3 litres cold water
1 carrot
1 turnip
1 onion (brown-skinned)
2 outside sticks celery
Bouquet garni
1 dozen peppercorns
1 dozen cloves
1 blade mace

1. Trim and wash the bones, remove the fat and marrow, and gash meat well.
2. Put bones, salt, meat, and water into the stock pot or saucepan.
3. Allow to soak $\frac{1}{2}$ to 1 hour.
4. Bring very slowly to simmering point with lid on saucepan.
5. Prepare the vegetables and cut up roughly; leave brown skin on the onion.
6. Add vegetables, bouquet garni, peppercorns, cloves, and mace.
7. Simmer gently $4\frac{1}{2}$ hours in saucepan, or about 30 minutes in a pressure cooker.
8. Remove bones and strain.
9. Allow to cool and remove the fat.

Economical stock

Water in which fresh meat or vegetables has been boiled may be used as a foundation for many soups.

FISH STOCK

1 kg fish or fish bones
12 peppercorns
3 sprigs parsley
Rind of 1 lemon
1 onion
1 blade mace
1 tablespoon salt
$2\frac{1}{2}$ litres water

1. Put all ingredients into a saucepan.
2. Bring slowly to the boil.
3. Boil slowly 1 hour with lid on saucepan.
4. Strain.

BROTH

500 g scrag end of mutton,
    beef bones or knuckle
    of veal
5 cups water
2 teaspoons salt
Pinch pepper
2 tablespoons pearl barley
1 carrot
1 onion
1 turnip (small)
2 sticks celery
2 tablespoons chopped
    parsley

1. Wash meat.
2. Cut the meat off the bones, and remove fat.
3. Cut the meat into small pieces.
4. Put meat and bones into a saucepan with water and salt and pepper.
5. Wash the barley well in cold water, and add to saucepan.
6. Bring slowly to simmering point to extract the juices and flavour from the meat.
7. Wash and prepare the vegetables, and cut into small dice, and add them to the broth.
8. Simmer slowly 2 or 3 hours with lid on saucepan.
9. Take out the bones.
10. Remove fat with a spoon and absorb the remainder with pieces of kitchen paper laid on the surface.
11. Add finely chopped parsley.
12. Serve hot.

JULIENNE SOUP

1 carrot
1 turnip
$\frac{1}{2}$ head celery
5 cups stock or clear soup
1 tablespoon arrowroot
Caramel
Salt if necessary

1. Wash and prepare the vegetables and peel or scrape according to their requirements.
2. Cut into thin strips like matches.
3. Cook the vegetables for 10 minutes in a little of the boiling stock or water.
4. Drain the vegetables, when tender, in a colander.
5. Heat the remaining stock.
6. Mix the arrowroot with a little cold water.
7. Stir into the stock and stir till boiling.
8. Allow to cook for 3 or 4 minutes.
9. Add a little caramel if necessary.
10. Add cooked vegetables and salt if required, and serve.

Soup cubes may be used for making stock.

LENTIL OR PEA SOUP

1 cup split peas or lentils
3 litres water
Some bacon bones or rind
1 teaspoon salt
12 peppercorns
9 cloves
1 blade mace
1 large carrot
1 large turnip
1 onion
½ head celery
1 teaspoon dried mint
4 tablespoons flour

1. Soak the peas or lentils overnight in some of the cold water.
2. Place them in a large saucepan with the bacon, salt, peppercorns, cloves, mace, and remaining water.
3. Bring slowly to the boil.
4. Prepare the vegetables; grate them or slice thinly.
5. Add to saucepan and cook slowly 3 hours with lid on.
6. Rub through a coarse strainer, a cupful at a time.
7. Return to saucepan, a   the dried mint, and bring to the boil.
8. Blend the flour smoothly with cold water.
9. Add to soup and stir until boiling.
10. Serve hot with small croutons of toast.

MINESTRONE

1 cup dried beans (navy or haricot)
2½ cups cold water
2 bacon rashers
Small clove garlic, finely chopped
1 medium onion chopped
1½ cups diced carrots
1 cup diced celery
1 cup diced green pepper
2 teaspoons salt
¼ teaspoon pepper
5 cups stock or water
1 cup tomato pulp
½ teaspoon mixed herbs
1 tablespoon chopped parsley
1 cup finely shredded cabbage
½ cup green peas
⅓ cup cooked macaroni

1. Soak beans in cold water overnight.
2. Remove rind from bacon, cut bacon into strips and fry in a large saucepan. Remove from saucepan.
3. Add finely chopped garlic and onion, carrots, celery, green pepper to saucepan. Fry in bacon fat, stirring well for about 5 minutes—do not brown.
4. Add beans and water in which they have been soaking, salt, pepper, stock, tomato pulp, herbs.
5. Simmer 2 hours with lid on saucepan.
6. Add remaining ingredients except bacon.
7. Simmer again 30 minutes.
8. Serve garnished with fried bacon.

MULLIGATAWNY SOUP

1 apple
1 onion
2 tablespoons butter or clear
    fat
1 tablespoon curry powder
1 tablespoon chutney
2 teaspoons sugar
$\frac{1}{4}$ cup lemon juice
2 tablespoons flour
2 litres stock
1 cup cooked rice

1. Prepare apple and onion and cut roughly.
2. Fry in butter or fat.
3. Add curry powder, chutney, sugar and lemon juice—cook gently 10 minutes.
4. Blend flour with a little stock, add with rest of stock and simmer gently 1 hour.
5. Rub through a strainer, return to saucepan and reheat.
6. Serve rice in the soup or separately.

OYSTER SOUP

3 dozen oysters
2 litres fish stock (see p. 6)
Strip thinly peeled lemon rind
1 blade mace
Salt to taste
$\frac{1}{4}$ cup butter
$\frac{1}{2}$ cup plain flour
$2\frac{1}{2}$ cups milk or $\frac{2}{3}$ cup cream
Cayenne to taste
Squeeze of lemon juice
1 teaspoon anchovy sauce

1. Beard or trim the oysters.
2. Put beards into stock with lemon rind, mace, and salt.
3. Simmer $\frac{1}{2}$ hour.
4. Strain.
5. Melt butter.
6. Stir the flour into the melted butter, off the stove.
7. Stir until smooth.
8. Cook 1 minute.
9. Add stock.
10. Stir till it boils.
11. Add milk or cream.
12. Reheat, but do not allow to boil if cream is used, as it will curdle.
13. Add cayenne, lemon juice, and anchovy sauce.
14. Put oysters into a gravy strainer.
15. Boil oyster liquor and hold strainer containing oysters in boiling liquor for 5 seconds.
16 Put oysters into serving dishes.
17. Pour the soup over.

TOMATO CREAM SOUP

12 tomatoes or 1 large tin tomatoes
1 white onion
2½ cups stock or water
1 teaspoon salt
Bunch of herbs
Bacon bone or rinds
1¼ cups thin melted butter sauce (see p. 144)
⅔ cup cream (optional)

1. Slice tomatoes and cut onion finely.
2. Put in saucepan with stock, salt, herbs and bacon.
3. Cook till onion is tender with lid on saucepan.
4. Rub through a strainer.
5. Gradually add this tomato puree to melted butter sauce and stir over low heat till hot but do not boil.
6. Add cream if liked. Add pepper to flavour as desired.
7. Serve with croutons.

VEGETABLE CREAM SOUP

4 medium potatoes
1 onion
½ head celery
1 parsnip
1 turnip
2 tablespoons butter
2 teaspoons sugar
2 teaspoons salt
5 cups water
2½ cups milk
2 tablespoons flour
Salt and pepper to taste

Note: A choice of vegetables may be used instead of all white.

1. Wash vegetables.
2. Peel and cut up roughly.
3. Make butter hot in saucepan.
4. Add vegetables.
5. Stir until they steam.
6. Add sugar, salt, and water.
7. Boil gently 1 hour or until tender.
8. Rub through a sieve or strainer.
9. Return to the saucepan.
10. Add the milk, and allow to come to the boil.
11. Mix the flour with a little cold water until it is quite smooth.
12. Stir it into the soup, and stir till it boils.
13. Allow to cook 1 minute.
14. Season with salt and white pepper to taste.
15. Serve hot with small croutons of fried bread.

Note. After rubbing through strainer the pulp could be added to 1¼ cups thin melted butter sauce and heated before serving as soup.

FISH

TO FILLET A FISH

1. Clean and scale the fish.
2. Place on the fish-board or paper.
3. Make an incision (with a pair of scissors or sharp knife) around the neck, up the middle of the back, across the tail, and up the belly, keeping as close to the fins as possible.
4. Loosen the skin around the head, and with a cloth quickly draw it off, holding the fish firmly by the head and being careful not to tear the flesh. Do this on both sides.
5. Cut down the middle of the back with a sharp knife.
6. Cut the flesh cleanly from the backbone on both sides, keeping the knife as close to the bone as possible.
7. Remove the small bones along the sides of the fish separately.
8. Cut flesh into 3 or 4 pieces according to the size of fish.
9. Wash in cold water to which have been added salt and a little lemon juice or vinegar. Dry well.

Note. Fillets are now ready for grilling, steaming, or frying.

BAKED FISH

1 flathead, bream or jewfish
Lemon juice
1 cup breadcrumbs (fresh)
1 tablespoon chopped parsley
A little grated lemon rind and nutmeg
1 tablespoon butter
$\frac{1}{4}$ teaspoon salt
Pinch pepper
Milk

1. Clean, scale, wash and dry the fish.
2. Remove the eyes.
3. Cut off the fins, and trim the tail.
4. Rub over inside and out with lemon juice.
5. Mix the breadcrumbs with all the other ingredients except the milk and a little of the butter.
6. Fill the fish with a portion of this, and sew with cotton or fasten with a skewer.

(continued)

7. Grease a baking dish or line with greased paper or aluminium foil.
8. Place the fish in the dish and brush with milk.
9. Cover with remainder of seasoning, adding a few more breadcrumbs if necessary.
10. Put a few small pieces of butter on top.
11. Cover with greased paper or foil.
12. Bake in a moderate oven, 180°–200°C, for 20 to 30 minutes.
13. Test with a skewer in thick part near the head.
14. Place on a hot dish with seasoning.
15. Garnish with sections of lemon and parsley.

FRIED FISH

1 small fish or fillets
1 tablespoon flour
Pinch pepper
$\frac{1}{2}$ teaspoon salt
1 beaten egg or a little milk
Breadcrumbs
Enough melted fat to cover bottom of pan.

1. Clean, scale, wash, and dry the fish.
2. Remove fins and cut into suitable-sized pieces.
3. Roll in the flour, pepper, and salt.
4. Dip in beaten egg or milk, and roll in breadcrumbs, pressing them on firmly.
5. Heat fat slowly until a fume begins to rise.
6. Place the fish in pan and fry for 1 minute on each side.
7. Cook slowly 10 to 15 minutes. Turn once.
8. Drain on absorbent paper.
9. Serve on a hot dish.
10. Garnish with slices of lemon and small sprigs of parsley.

GRILLED FISH

1 small fish or fillets
Butter
Salt
Pepper

1. Clean and scale the fish.
2. Remove head and fins, split open.
3. Wash and dry.
4. Grill lightly on both sides.
5. Cook from 5 to 8 minutes according to thickness (try with a skewer in the thickest part to determine if it is tender).
6. Serve at once on a hot plate.
7. Flavour with butter, salt, and pepper.
8. Garnish with lemon juice and finely chopped parsley.

Minestrone Soup (p. 8).

STEAMED FISH

1 fish or fillets
Juice of 1 lemon
Salt and cayenne pepper
$\frac{2}{3}$ cup masking sauce (see p. 144)

1. Clean, scale, wash and dry the fish; remove fins and trim the tail.
2. Wash in water to which have been added salt and a teaspoon of lemon juice (or a little vinegar).
3. Wipe dry.
4. Place on a greased plate.
5. Sprinkle salt, cayenne, and remainder of lemon juice over fish.
6. Cover with another greased plate.
7. Place over a saucepan of gently boiling water.
8. Steam 10 minutes or until tender.
9. Lift onto a hot dish.
10. Cover the fish with the prepared sauce, to which has been added any liquor on the plate.
11. Garnish with lemon and parsley.

FISH CAKES

4 medium potatoes (boiled)
500 g cooked fish
Salt and pepper to taste
1½ tablespoons butter
Little grated lemon rind
1 tablespoon chopped parsley
1 egg
1 tablespoon flour
Breadcrumbs
Fat for frying

1. Mash potatoes finely.
2. Break up fish, removing bones.
3. Mix together, and add salt, pepper, butter, lemon rind, parsley, and 1 well-beaten egg.
4. Form small amounts of the mixture into balls, firming well in flour. Flatten on a board by pressing top and sides with a large knife.
5. Brush over with beaten egg.
6. Shake in breadcrumbs, pressing them on well.
7. Fry for 3 minutes in hot fat till a golden-brown colour.
8. Drain on absorbent paper.
9. Serve on a hot dish.
10. Garnish with lemon wedges and sprigs of parsley.

Note. A small can of salmon or tuna may be used instead of fresh fish.

Baked Fish (p. 11) with green peas (p. 40) and baby carrots (p. 38).

FISH CREAM

1 cup cooked fish
1 egg
$\frac{2}{3}$ cup masking sauce (see p. 144)
Few drops lemon juice
1 tablespoon fresh bread-crumbs

1. Flake fish.
2. Separate yolk from white of egg.
3. Mix all ingredients well except egg white.
4. Beat white stiffly and fold in.
5. Put into well-greased mould.
6. Cover with greased paper.
7. Steam 15 minutes.
8. Turn onto a hot dish.
9. Garnish with lemon and parsley.

SCALLOPED FISH

1. Make up recipe for fish cream (above).
2. Prepare scallop shell by greasing with butter and sprinkling with breadcrumbs.
3. Place in the prepared mixture, sprinkle bread-crumbs on top.
4. Add a few pieces of butter and brown lightly in the oven or under a griller.

SCALLOPED OYSTERS

1 dozen oysters
$\frac{2}{3}$ cup milk
1 tablespoon butter
Salt and cayenne pepper to taste
1 tablespoon flour
Fine breadcrumbs
Good squeeze lemon juice

1. Beard or trim oysters and simmer beards in milk for 3 minutes.
2. Strain and allow to cool.
3. Melt butter.
4. Add the flour off the heat, stir till smooth, then return to heat.
5. Add liquid, and stir until it boils and thickens. Add oysters.
6. Thickly grease some scallop shells with butter, sprinkle with breadcrumbs, then add oyster mixture, to which has been added the lemon juice, salt, and cayenne.
7. Sprinkle a few crumbs on each, and place a piece of butter on top.
8. Stand in oven or under griller until lightly browned.
9. Serve hot, and garnish with parsley and lemon.

FISH PIES

1 cup cooked fish
$\frac{2}{3}$ cup masking sauce, which may be made with fish stock instead of milk (see p. 144).
1 tablespoon chopped parsley
$\frac{1}{2}$ teaspoon anchovy sauce
Squeeze of lemon juice
Salt and pepper or cayenne pepper to taste
2 quantities flaky pastry or shortcrust pastry (see pp. 92, 93).
1 beaten egg (or a little milk) for glazing

1. Carefully remove skin and bone from fish.
2. Chop up fish rather small.
3. Add it to the white sauce, with chopped parsley, anchovy sauce, and other flavourings.
4. Mix well together.
5. Roll out the pastry about 3 mm thick.
6. Stamp out with round cutters, one the size of the top of the patty tins, and one two sizes larger for the bottom pieces; cut top pieces first.
7. Line plain patty tins with the larger pieces of pastry.
8. Fill the pastry cases equally with the fish mixture.
9. Wet edges of pastry with water.
10. Place top pieces on, and glaze with egg or milk.
11. Bake in a hot oven, $220°–250°C$, for about 20 minutes.
12. Serve on a hot dish.
13. Garnish with lemon, and sprigs of parsley.

Note. A small can of salmon or tuna may be used instead of fresh fish.

SALMON MAYONNAISE

1 cucumber
Tomatoes or beetroot
1 lettuce
1 can (250 g) salmon
Salt and pepper to flavour
$1\frac{1}{4}$ cups mayonnaise or salad dressing (see pp. 45, 46).

1. Prepare vegetables.
2. Arrange in bowl.
3. Place a portion of salmon on each curly lettuce leaf. Flavour with salt and pepper.
4. Mask salmon with mayonnaise (or the mayonnaise may be served separately in a small jug).
5. Garnish with radishes and celery curls.

SCOTCH HADDOCK OR SMOKED COD

250 g haddock or cod
Juice of 1 lemon
1 blade mace (optional)
1 teaspoon butter
1 cup melted butter sauce (see
    p. 144).

1. Cut fish into suitably sized pieces.
2. Place in a pan or saucepan, cover with cold water, bring to boil, and simmer for 5 minutes.
3. Drain off the water.
4. Squeeze the lemon juice over the fish, add mace and a small piece of butter.
5. Cover closely and heat gently for 10 to 15 minutes.
6. Serve plain or with melted butter sauce.
7. Garnish with parsley.

MEAT AND POULTRY DISHES

ABERDEEN SAUSAGE

500 g bladebone or round
    steak
250 g fat bacon, rind removed
1 cup fresh breadcrumbs
$\frac{1}{2}$ teaspoon salt
Pinch pepper
1 egg
1 tablespoon tomato sauce
1 tablespoon Worcestershire
    sauce
$\frac{1}{2}$ cup brown breadcrumbs
    for rolling

1. Have boiling water in readiness.
2. Cut the meat and bacon up finely, add the breadcrumbs, salt and pepper.
3. Beat the egg, add to it the two sauces, and mix with the other ingredients.
4. Press into a roll like a thick sausage; tie it up in a floured pudding cloth for boiling, or in aluminium foil for steaming.
5. Boil or steam for $2\frac{1}{4}$ hours; leave until cold, then roll in breadcrumbs.
6. Serve cold, sliced thinly, and garnished with sprigs of parsley.

BEEF OLIVES

500 g round or topside steak
4 tablespoons breadcrumbs
2 teaspoons chopped parsley
1 teaspoon each chopped
    thyme and marjoram
$\frac{1}{2}$ teaspoon salt
Pinch pepper
1 tablespoon butter, chopped
    suet, or clarified fat
Grated nutmeg
6 drops lemon juice
1 tablespoon fat
$1\frac{1}{4}$ cups water
2 tablespoons plain flour

1. Wipe steak with a damp cloth, and cut off all fat.
2. Cut steak in pieces about 10 cm square.
3. Mix together breadcrumbs, chopped parsley, thyme, marjoram, salt, pepper, butter or suet, nutmeg, and lemon juice.
4. Place a little mixture on each piece of steak, roll steak up and tie firmly with white string or cotton.
5. Heat fat in a saucepan, and fry rolls of meat until browned; pour fat away.
6. Put meat, salt, pepper, and water in saucepan, simmer very gently for 2 hours or until meat is quite tender.
7. Take out olives, remove string, and place meat on a hot meat dish.

(continued)

8. Blend flour with a little cold water, add it to the meat juices, stir till boiling, and simmer gently for 5 minutes. Reheat the olives and serve with the gravy on a hot dish.

GRILLED BACON ROLLS

4 bacon rashers, thinly sliced

1. Cut rind off bacon, and cut bacon into 5 cm lengths.
2. Roll and thread loosely on a skewer.
3. Grill gently until fat is clear, about 5 minutes.

CORNED BEEF

1 joint corned beef
1 teaspoon vinegar
6 cloves
12 peppercorns
1 blade mace
Carrots
Turnips
Suet crust (see p. 94).

1. Wash the joint to remove some of the salt.
2. Weigh, and allow at least 40 minutes' cooking time for each 500 g.
3. Place the joint in a saucepan of warm water, and bring to simmering point.
4. Add vinegar, cloves, peppercorns, and mace.
5. Carrots, turnips, and suet dumplings may be cooked in the water with the meat: vegetables 30 minutes; dumplings (balls of suet crust) 20 minutes.
7. Serve on a hot plate with parsley, mustard, or onion sauce as an accompaniment (see p. 144).
8. If serving cold, allow the meat to cool in the water in which it has been cooked.

A pressure cooker can be used for corned beef to reduce cooking time.

ROAST BEEF

1. Prepare oven.
2. Wipe the joint over with a damp cloth.
3. Weigh joint and allow 30 minutes' cooking time for each 500 g.
4. Place in baking dish. Add 1 to 2 tablespoons of fat if very lean.
5. Place in a moderate oven, $180°–200°$C, and cook gently for the required time.

(continued)

6. Bake vegetables under and around the joint for 40 to 45 minutes (see p. 36).
7. When cooked, serve on a hot plate, accompanied by Yorkshire pudding (see p. 90), horse-radish sauce (see p. 142), and brown gravy (see p. 140).

FRIED BRAINS AND BACON

2 sets brains
1 small piece onion
2 sage leaves
1 egg
1 tablespoon plain flour
$\frac{1}{4}$ teaspoon salt
Pinch pepper
2 tablespoons breadcrumbs
Enough fat to cover bottom of pan when melted
2 slices of fat bacon

1. Wash and remove the skin from the brains.
2. Place in a saucepan with onion and sage, and cover with water.
3. Bring to simmering point and simmer for 6 minutes.
4. Place on a plate, allow to cool, and cut in four.
5. Beat the egg in a deep plate.
6. Mix flour, salt, and pepper together on a plate, and place the breadcrumbs on a sheet of white paper.
7. Roll the brains in the seasoned flour, brush with egg, and toss in breadcrumbs, pressing crumbs on firmly with a knife.
8. Heat fat slowly until a fume begins to rise.
9. Fry brains for 1 minute on each side, then cook gently for 3 minutes on each side. Drain on absorbent paper.
10. Remove rind from bacon, cut in 5 cm pieces, roll and place loosely on a skewer, then grill till the fat is transparent.
11. Serve brains and bacon on a hot dish, garnished with sprigs of parsley.

BAKED CHICKEN

1 chicken
1 cup stuffing (see p. 166).
4 slices fat bacon
Brown gravy (see p. 140).

1. Wash chicken thoroughly.
2. Fill with stuffing.
3. Truss or tie into a neat shape.
4. Cover with greased brown paper or foil.
5. Bake in a moderate oven, 180°–200°C, for 1½ hours or until tender.
6. Serve with grilled bacon, brown gravy and baked vegetables (see p. 36).

Note. Rabbit may be cooked by this method.

CHICKEN OR RABBIT PIE

1 chicken or rabbit
2 tablespoons plain flour
$\frac{1}{2}$ teaspoon salt
Pinch pepper
1 onion
2 cups stock or water
2 hard-cooked eggs
2 slices bacon, rind removed
2 tablespoons chopped parsley
$1\frac{1}{2}$ quantities flaky or short-crust pastry (see pp. 92, 93).

1. Wash chicken or rabbit thoroughly and cut into neat joints.
2. Mix together the flour, salt, and pepper on a plate.
3. Roll joints in seasoned flour.
4. Place in saucepan with onion; add stock or water and simmer $1\frac{1}{2}$ hours or until tender.
5. Turn into pie-dish to cool. Add sliced hard-cooked eggs, bacon and chopped parsley.
6. Roll out pastry in the shape of the pie-dish with 2.5 cm extra all round.
7. Cut a narrow strip from the edge of the pastry, and lay it on the wet rim of the pie-dish with the cut edge outside.
8. Brush with milk.
9. Place the remainder of the pastry over the top of the pie, making sure the narrow strip on the pie-dish is completely covered.
10. Trim the edges with a sharp knife.
11. Ornament the top with a rose and leaves cut from the pastry leftovers.
12. Glaze by brushing with milk or yolk of egg.
13. Bake in a hot oven, $220°-250°C$, for 20 minutes.

GRILLED CHOPS

4 short loin chops, 2.5 cm thick
2 teaspoons butter
Salt and pepper

1. Remove skin (but not the fat) from chops.
2. Make into neat shapes, and fasten with sharpened match-sticks.
3. Grease bars of gridiron.
4. Grill under moderate heat and allow to cook for from 10 to 15 minutes, according to taste and thickness of meat, turning every 3 minutes.
5. Remove match-sticks, and put on a hot dish.
6. Flavour with butter, salt, and pepper.
7. Serve at once.

HARICOT CHOPS OR STEAK

500 g neck chops or round or
    bladebone steak
1 medium-sized onion
1 tablespoon clarified fat
3 tablespoons plain flour
$\frac{1}{2}$ teaspoon salt
Pinch pepper
$1\frac{1}{4}$ cups water or stock
1 carrot
1 turnip
1 stick celery
1 tablespoon parsley

1. Trim meat and remove excess fat.
2. Peel onion; slice into rings, or dice.
3. Melt fat in saucepan. Brown meat, and remove from saucepan; brown onion and remove from saucepan.
4. Add flour, salt, and pepper; allow to brown.
5. Add water and stir till simmering.
6. Add meat and onion and simmer gently 1 hour.
7. Prepare vegetables, cut into rings or large dice.
8. Add vegetables to haricot and simmer all gently 1 hour longer.
9. Serve on a hot plate and sprinkle with chopped parsley.

CORNISH PASTIES

250 g round (or minced) steak
1 potato
1 onion
1 tablespoon chopped parsley
1 teaspoon salt
Pinch pepper
Double quantity shortcrust
    pastry (see p. 93)
Egg or milk for glazing

1. Dice meat.
2. Peel potato and onion, wash and wipe dry, and dice.
3. Mix together the meat, potato, and onion with parsley, salt, and pepper.
4. Divide into 6 or 8 equal parts.
5. Heat the oven to 220°–260° C.
6. Knead shortcrust till smooth.
7. Cut into 6 or 8 even pieces, and roll out each piece into a circle.
8. Place one heap of the meat and vegetable mixture on each piece of pastry.
9. Wet edges of pastry halfway round with water.
10. Turn into a half-moon shape, and join pastry edges together by pinching a small neat frill.
11. Place on a flat tin.
12. Glaze with egg or milk.
13. Bake in hot oven, 220°–260°C, for 10 minutes, and then reduce heat to 120°–160°C, for 20 minutes longer.
14. Serve garnished with sprigs of parsley, and accompanied by tomato or brown sauce (see pp. 148, 141).

CRUMBED FRIED CUTLETS

5 cutlets
2 tablespoons plain flour
½ teaspoon salt
Pinch pepper
1 egg
1 tablespoon milk
1 cup breadcrumbs
Enough fat to cover bottom
of pan when melted

1. Remove skin and gristle from cutlets and trim nicely, leaving about 5 cm of bare bone.
2. Mix flour, salt, and pepper on a plate.
3. Beat egg on a plate. Add milk.
4. Spread breadcrumbs on white paper.
5. Dip cutlets in seasoned flour, brush with beaten egg and milk, and toss in breadcrumbs, pressing them on firmly with a knife.
6. Heat fat, add cutlets, fry gently 1 minute on each side, then cook gently for 10 to 15 minutes, turning once.
7. Drain cutlets on absorbent paper.
8. Have ready a mound of mashed potatoes on a hot plate, and place cutlets around it with the bones pointing upwards.
9. Serve with brown, tomato, or onion sauce (see pp. 141, 148, 144).

GRILLED OR FRENCH CUTLETS

1. Trim cutlets, leaving 2.5 cm of bare bone.
2. Grease gridiron.
3. Grill under moderate heat 7 to 10 minutes, turning once.
4. On hot plates serve cutlets dotted with a little green butter (see p. 165) and accompanied by chips (see p. 41) and bacon rolls (see p. 18).

DRY CURRY

1 apple
1 onion
1 tomato
2 tablespoons butter or
substitute
½ tablespoon curry powder
500g tender steak or veal

1. Cut the apple, onion, and tomato into dice.
2. Place in a saucepan with the butter and curry powder.
3. Fry without browning for 10 minutes.
4. Cut the meat into small dice; add to saucepan with the chutney, jam, sultanas, sugar, sliced banana, and coconut.

(continued)

1 tablespoon chutney
1 tablespoon jam
1 tablespoon sultanas
1 tablespoon sugar
1 banana
2 tablespoons desiccated
    coconut
1 tablespoon lemon juice
$\frac{1}{2}$ teaspoon salt

5. Simmer very gently for about 1 hour or till the meat is very tender.
6. Half an hour before serving add the lemon juice and salt.
7. Serve with boiled rice (see p. 5).

CURRIED CHOPS OR STEAK

750 g neck chops, or round or
    bladebone steak
1 apple
1 onion
1 tablespoon dripping
1 tablespoon plain flour
1 tablespoon curry powder
1 teaspoon salt
2 teaspoons sugar
$2\frac{1}{2}$ cups stock or water

1. Wipe meat with a damp cloth.
2. Remove skin and excess fat.
3. Prepare apple and onion, and mince finely.
4. Heat dripping and fry apple and onion till brown.
5. Add flour, curry powder, salt, and sugar. Stir well.
6. Add stock or water and stir till boiling.
7. Add meat and simmer $1\frac{1}{2}$ to 2 hours.
8. Skim off fat.
9. Serve on hot plate with border of boiled rice (see p. 5) and slices of lemon.
10. Garnish with parsley.

GOULASH

500 g round or topside steak
1 tablespoon plain flour
1 medium onion
1 tablespoon butter
1 cup stock or tomato puree
1 small clove garlic
1 teaspoon paprika
$\frac{1}{2}$ teaspoon salt
Pinch pepper
1 potato

1. Cut meat into cubes and roll in flour.
2. Peel and slice onion.
3. Lightly brown onion in melted butter. Add steak and brown.
4. Add stock or puree, and all other ingredients except potato.
5. Cover and simmer about $1\frac{1}{2}$ hours.
6. Cut potato into cubes and place on steak. Simmer for another 20 to 30 minutes, or until potato is cooked.
7. Serve on hot plates.

IRISH STEW

4 neck chops
2 tablespoons flour
$\frac{1}{2}$ teaspoon salt
Pinch pepper
$1\frac{1}{4}$ cups water
4 potatoes
1 onion

1. Wipe chops with a damp cloth, and remove skin, gristle, and fat.
2. Mix flour, salt, and pepper on a plate.
3. Dip each chop in seasoned flour.
4. Place a little water in a saucepan and pack chops into it. Sprinkle any remaining seasoned flour over the chops, add the remainder of the water and bring quickly to simmering point.
5. Cook gently 45 minutes.
6. Prepare the vegetables.
7. Cut potatoes into pieces about 5 cm square, or rings 2.5 cm thick; slice onions into thin rings.
8. Place onions on meat, potatoes on top; allow to simmer gently 1 hour longer.
9. Serve on a hot plate, first lifting potatoes out then chops. Pour gravy over.

BONED SHOULDER OF LAMB OR MUTTON

1 shoulder of lamb or mutton (boned)

Stuffing
1 cup fresh breadcrumbs
1 tablespoon butter or finely chopped suet
$\frac{1}{4}$ teaspoon salt
Pinch pepper
1 tablespoon chopped parsley
$\frac{1}{2}$ teaspoon each chopped thyme and chopped marjoram (or pinch dried herbs)
A little grated nutmeg or lemon rind
1 egg or 2 tablespoons milk

1. Wipe meat with damp cloth and trim it.
2. Mix all stuffing ingredients together and moisten with egg or milk.
3. Fill meat with stuffing and sew up or tie.
4. Weigh joint and allow 30 minutes' cooking time for each 500 g.
5. Place in baking dish fat side up (if very lean add 1 or 2 tablespoons of fat).
6. Place in moderate oven and cook slowly for required length of time.
7. Make stock for gravy by simmering bone in $1\frac{1}{4}$ cups water.
8. Turn meat when half cooked.
9. Vegetables such as potatoes or pumpkin may be baked with meat. Allow from $\frac{3}{4}$ to 1 hour for these to cook.

(continued)

10. When meat and vegetables are done, lift meat onto a hot serving dish and remove cotton or string used for sewing.
11. Drain vegetables on absorbent paper and sprinkle with salt and pepper.
12. Keep hot while making thin brown gravy, and serve.

Thin Brown Gravy
Pour off almost all the fat from baking dish, sprinkle in 2 teaspoons plain flour, and allow to brown; add $\frac{2}{3}$ cup stock (made from bone out of shoulder), and stir till boiling.

FRICASSEED LAMB, CHICKEN, OR RABBIT

250 g neck chops or chicken or rabbit
1 small onion
$\frac{1}{2}$ teaspoon salt
Pinch pepper
1 tablespoon plain flour
$\frac{1}{2}$ cup milk

1. Wipe meat with a damp cloth.
2. Trim fat and marrow from chops, keeping a neat shape.
3. Dice onion.
4. Put meat and onion into a saucepan with sufficient water to barely cover them.
5. Add salt and pepper, bring to the boil, then simmer gently $1\frac{1}{2}$ hours.
6. Blend flour smoothly with a little milk.
7. Remove meat and onion from saucepan and measure liquid.
8. Return $\frac{1}{3}$ cup of liquid to saucepan and add remaining milk.
9. Stir blended flour in carefully, return meat and onion to saucepan, and cook 3 minutes.
10. Serve on a hot dish, and garnish with parsley.

ROAST LAMB

1. Follow directions for Roast Mutton (see p. 27), but allow 20 to 25 minutes cooking time to each 500 g.
2. Serve meat and vegetables with thin brown gravy (see above) and mint sauce (see p. 143).

CROWN ROAST OF LAMB

12–16 rib chops prepared by butcher for a crown roast (prepared as for cutlets but left in one piece).

1. Form chops into a circle and tie securely.
2. Place in a greased baking dish.
3. Cover chop ends with greaseproof paper or aluminium foil to prevent burning.
4. Bake in a moderate oven, 180°–200° C, allowing 20 minutes for each 500 g.
5. Serve on a hot plate.

Note. The centre of the crown may be partly filled with stuffing before cooking, or, if the roast is to be served at table, cooked vegetables such as green peas and diced carrots may be placed in the centre.

LIVER AND BACON

1 lamb's fry
2 tablespoons flour
$\frac{1}{2}$ teaspoon salt
Pinch pepper
Enough fat to cover bottom of pan when melted
250 g fat bacon
2 cups water

1. Wash liver well.
2. Dry liver and cut downwards in slices about 1 cm thick.
3. Mix flour, salt, and pepper on a plate; coat each slice of liver in seasoned flour.
4. Heat fat in frying pan.
5. Fry slices of liver slowly for 8 to 10 minutes, turning frequently.
6. Remove liver, drain on absorbent paper, and pour nearly all the fat out of frying-pan.
7. Cook bacon, remove, and keep hot.
8. Sprinkle remainder of seasoned flour into frying-pan. Stir well until browned, add water, and stir until boiling.
9. Strain gravy if necessary and return to pan; add fried liver, and simmer gently 7 to 10 minutes.
10. Serve liver and gravy on a hot plate, and garnish with bacon and chopped parsley.

GRILLED MINCE ROLL

500 g (1¾ cups) minced steak
1 cup soft breadcrumbs
1 cup grated cheese

1. Press steak into a rectangle on greaseproof paper or polythene.
2. Mix all other ingredients.

(continued)

1 tablespoon chopped parsley
1 onion, finely chopped
Salt and pepper to taste
$\frac{1}{2}$ cup plum or tomato sauce
    (see pp. 147, 148).

3. Spread onto minced steak.
4. Roll lengthways. Chill thoroughly.
5. Cut into 1 cm thick slices.
6. Grill 10 to 12 minutes.
7. Serve on hot plates.

SIMMERED FRESH MUTTON OR PUMPED LEG

1. Place a saucepan of water on to boil.
2. Trim mutton if necessary.
3. Weigh meat, and allow at least 30 minutes' cooking time for each 500 g.
4. Place thick side downward in the saucepan.
5. Simmer gently until tender. (Carrots and turnips may be boiled with it, cooking them about $\frac{3}{4}$ hour).
6. Serve on a hot dish accompanied by parsley, onion, or caper sauce (see pp. 144, 145).
7. When the water is cold, remove fat from top. This liquid may then be used in the making of broths and gravies, if fresh meat has been used.

ROAST MUTTON (LEG OR SHOULDER)

1. Prepare oven.
2. Wipe the joint over with a damp cloth and remove knuckle.
3. Weigh the joint and allow 30 minutes' cooking time for each 500 g.
4. Place in a baking dish fat side up. If lean, add 1 or 2 tablespoons fat.
5. Place into a moderate oven, 180°–200°C. Cook gently for the required time.
6. Bake vegetables in the dish for 40 to 45 minutes (see p. 36).
7. When cooked, serve meat and vegetables on a hot plate, accompanied by red currant jelly and brown gravy (see p. 140).

STEWED OXTAIL

1 oxtail
2 tablespoons plain flour
1 teaspoon salt
Pinch pepper
1 onion
1 tablespoon fat
1 bouquet garni
6 peppercorns
1 blade of mace
1 dessertspoon sugar
4 cups stock or water
1 carrot
1 turnip

1. Wash oxtail well; dry.
2. Cut into neat joints, removing as much fat as possible, and roll on flour, salt, and pepper.
3. Peel and slice onion.
4. Melt fat in a saucepan and fry meat till brown. Remove from saucepan.
5. Brown onion, then return meat to the saucepan and add bouquet garni, peppercorns, mace, sugar and stock or water.
6. Bring to simmering point and simmer for 3 hours.
7. Remove all fat with a spoon.
8. Wash, peel, and slice carrot and turnip and add to the other ingredients.
9. Simmer 1 hour longer.
10. Serve on a hot plate.

Note. It is better to cook this dish one day ahead and remove fat when cold. A pressure cooker can be used to reduce cooking time.

ROAST PORK

1. Prepare oven.
2. Wipe the joint over with a damp cloth, and score the rind.
3. Weigh the joint and allow 40 minutes to each 500 g.
4. Season joint if desired with sage and onion seasoning.
5. Place in a baking dish fat side up.
6. Cover with aluminium foil or greaseproof paper, and cook gently in a moderate oven, 180°–200° C, for the required time. Remove foil or greaseproof paper 30 minutes before serving.
7. Cook vegetables for 40 to 45 minutes under and around the joint (see p. 36).
8. Drain pork and vegetables on absorbent paper, and serve on hot plates, accompanied by thick brown gravy and apple sauce (see p. 140).

Roast Rack of Lamb. Cook as for Crown Roast of Lamb (p. 26).

POT ROAST

1 rolled roast
2 tablespoons plain flour
$\frac{1}{2}$ teaspoon salt
Pinch pepper
Vegetables
Enough fat to cover the
      bottom of saucepan
      when melted

1. Choose a heavy saucepan large enough to hold joint and vegetables.
2. Weigh joint and allow 30 minutes' cooking time for each 500 g.
3. Mix flour, salt and pepper, and rub well over joint.
4. Prepare vegetables.
5. Melt fat in saucepan.
6. Brown joint. Remove from saucepan.
7. Brown vegetables. Remove.
8. Return meat to saucepan, and cover with a tightly fitting lid.
9. Cook gently for the required time.
10. Return vegetables to saucepan, placing them around the meat, 40 minutes before serving time.
11. Drain on absorbent paper and serve on a hot plate.

FRIED SAUSAGES

6 sausages
2 tablespoons plain flour
$\frac{1}{2}$ teaspoon salt
Pinch pepper
Enough fat to cover the
      bottom of pan when
      melted
$1\frac{1}{4}$ cups water

1. Prick sausages with a fork.
2. Mix flour, salt, and pepper on a plate.
3. Dip sausages in seasoned flour.
4. Heat fat, and fry sausages gently until nicely browned, about 20 minutes, turning every 5 minutes.
5. Drain sausages on absorbent paper.
6. Pour nearly all the fat out of pan, add remaining seasoned flour, and stir until browned; add water and stir until boiling.
7. Serve sausages with strained gravy on a hot plate.

Chicken Pie (p. 20) with sweet corn (p. 42) and
(uncooked) globe artichokes.

SAUSAGE ROLLS

250 g ($\frac{3}{4}$ cup) mince or sausage
    meat
1 tablespoon chopped parsley
1 tablespoon plain flour
$\frac{1}{2}$ teaspoon salt
Pinch pepper
$\frac{1}{4}$ cup water
1 quantity flaky or shortcrust
    pastry (see pp. 92, 93).
Egg or milk for glazing

1. Put the meat, parsley, flour, salt, pepper, and water into a saucepan and stir over heat for 5 minutes.
2. Turn onto a plate to cool.
3. Roll the pastry into a square 3 mm thick.
4. Cut a strip off all round, as cut edges rise better.
5. Divide the pastry, and also the meat, into 8 equal parts.
6. Place one portion of meat not quite in the centre of each piece of pastry.
7. Fold one side of pastry onto the meat.
8. Half overlap the other side.
9. Press ends and top together with the back of a knife.
10. Glaze by brushing with milk or egg.
11. Place on an oven slide.
12. Bake in a hot oven, 220°–260°C, for 15 to 20 minutes.
13. Serve on a hot plate, and garnish with small sprigs of parsley.

For small rolls

1. Roll pastry into a long strip 8 cm wide. Brush edges with water.
2. Pile meat along centre.
3. Fold one side of pastry onto meat and press well.
4. Brush folded side of pastry with water; fold other edge over the wet pastry and press lightly.
5. Place on a baking tray.
6. Cut partly through with a sharp knife to length required.
7. Bake at 220°–250°C for 15 to 20 minutes. Cut right through and serve.

SEA PIE

1 sheep's kidney
500 g steak
1 tablespoon flour
$\frac{1}{2}$ teaspoon salt
Pinch pepper
$2\frac{1}{2}$ cups water
1 teaspoon vinegar
1 small carrot
1 small turnip
1 small onion
$1\frac{1}{2}$ quantities suet crust, short-crust pastry, or scone dough (see pp. 94, 93, 128).

1. Wash and skin the kidneys.
2. Cut steak and kidney into small pieces.
3. Mix flour, salt, and pepper together, and roll the meat in it.
4. Put meat, water, and vinegar in a saucepan, bring to simmering point, and simmer 1 hour.
5. Prepare vegetables and cut into dice; add to saucepan and allow all to simmer gently $\frac{1}{2}$ hour.
6. Roll pastry or dough to the same size as the saucepan lid, place on meat, and cut an incision in the centre of the pastry. Put lid on saucepan and cook gently $\frac{1}{2}$ hour longer.
7. Cut pastry or dough into triangular pieces, lift out of saucepan, and serve on a hot plate with meat and vegetables.

GRILLED STEAK

Rump, fillet, sirloin, or T-bone steak.

1. Grease the bars of gridiron to prevent meat from sticking.
2. Grill meat under moderate heat, turning every 3 minutes.
3. Cook for about 12 to 15 minutes, according to individual taste and to thickness of meat.
4. Serve on a hot plate with parsley butter (green butter see p. 165) (or butter, pepper, and salt), and potato chips (see p. 41).

SHARP STEAK

1 kg topside or round steak
2 tablespoons flour
A little grated nutmeg
1 tablespoon brown sugar
1 teaspoon salt
A little cayenne pepper

1. Trim steak. Mix together flour, nutmeg, sugar, salt, and cayenne pepper, and rub well into steak.
2. Place in a deep flameproof dish or casserole; add water, vinegar, and sauces.
3. Cover with another dish or a lid.

(continued)

1¼ cups water
1 tablespoon vinegar
1 tablespoon Worcestershire
    sauce
1 tablespoon mushroom ket-
    chup or tomato sauce

4. Place in oven and cook slowly for 2 hours at 120°–160°C, after it reaches simmering point.
5. Lift steak onto a very hot dish or serve from casserole.
6. Serve garnished with gherkins cut in strips and a few capers.

STEAK AND KIDNEY PIE

250 g steak
1 sheep's kidney
1 tablespoon plain flour
½ teaspoon salt
Pinch pepper
1 quantity flaky or shortcrust
    pastry (see pp. 92, 93).
Egg yolk or milk for glazing

1. Cut steak into thin slices about 5 cm square.
2. Wash and skin kidney and cut into small pieces.
3. Mix flour, salt, and pepper on a plate and roll steak in it.
4. Place steak and kidney in a saucepan; add just enough water to cover.
5. Cook gently 1½ to 2 hours or until tender. Cool and place in a pie-dish.
6. Roll pastry out in the shape of the pie-dish, with 2.5 cm extra all round.
7. Wet the rim of the pie-dish with cold water.
8. Cut a narrow strip from the edge of the pastry, and place it on the wet rim of pie-dish, turning the cut edge to the outside, as cut edges rise better.
9. Moisten the strip with water, and put the remainder of the pastry over the top of the pie, making sure the strip on the pie-dish rim is completely covered.
10. Trim the edges with a sharp knife.
11. Ornament the top with a rose and leaves made from the pastry scraps.
12. Make 3 incisions in the pastry.
13. Glaze with yolk of egg or milk.
14. Bake in a hot oven, 220°–250°C, till the pastry is brown, about 20 minutes.

STEAK AND KIDNEY PUDDING

250 g steak
1 sheep's kidney
1 tablespoon flour
1 teaspoon chopped parsley
$\frac{1}{2}$ teaspoon salt
Pinch pepper
1 quantity suet crust (see p. 94)
$\frac{1}{2}$ cup water

1. Remove fat from meat and cut into 1 cm squares.
2. Wash and skin the kidney, and cut into small pieces.
3. Mix meat, kidney, flour, parsley, salt, and pepper on a plate.
4. Put a large saucepan of water on to boil.
5. Knead and roll out two-thirds of the pastry, and line a small pudding basin with it.
6. Fill with meat mixture, piling high in the middle; add water, and wet around edges of the pastry.
7. Knead and roll out remainder of pastry, lay across top of basin, and where pastry lining and top meet at rim, press edges together and pinch a frill.
8. Tie a floured cloth firmly over the basin with a piece of string, and knot the opposite corners of cloth.
9. Boil for 2 to $2\frac{1}{2}$ hours.
10. Remove cloth and string.
11. Serve on a hot plate.

Note. This pudding can be steamed; cover pastry with greaseproof paper or aluminium foil; place in a steamer or in a saucepan with water reaching half-way up the sides of the basin, and steam for $2\frac{1}{2}$ to 3 hours.

STEAK AND KIDNEY WITH SCONE TOPPING

500 g round or bladebone steak
2 sheep's kidneys
1 onion
1 carrot
1 tablespoon fat
1 tablespoon flour

1. Cut steak and kidney into convenient-size pieces.
2. Peel onion and cut into rings or dice.
3. Peel carrot and cut into rings or dice.
4. Heat fat in saucepan, add onion, and stir until it just changes colour.
5. Add flour, salt, and pepper; brown lightly.

(continued)

$\frac{1}{2}$ teaspoon salt
Pinch pepper
1 quantity plain scone mixture (see p. 128).
1 tablespoon chopped parsley

6. Add water and stir till boiling.
7. Add meat and simmer gently 1 hour.
8. Add carrot and simmer $\frac{1}{2}$ hour longer.
9. Make plain scones.
10. Arrange scones on top of stew, put lid on tightly and cook gently 20 minutes.
11. Serve on hot plates and sprinkle with finely chopped parsley.

SIMMERED SHEEP'S OR OX TONGUES

4 sheep's tongues or 1 ox tongue
3 cloves
1 blade mace (optional)

1. Wash tongues well.
2. Place cloves and mace in saucepan with enough water to cover tongues, and bring to boil.
3. Add tongues.
4. Simmer gently 2 to 3 hours or until tender.
5. Remove skins.
6. Serve hot with parsley sauce (see p. 144).
7. If to be served cold, press after removing skin.

A pressure cooker can be used for cooking tongues to reduce cooking time.

FRICASSEED TRIPE AND ONION

500 g tripe
$\frac{1}{2}$ teaspoon salt
1 white onion
1 tablespoon flour
$\frac{2}{3}$ cup milk
1 tablespoon butter
1 tablespoon chopped parsley

1. Wash the tripe (scrape the underside if necessary), and cut it into pieces 2 cm square.
2. Place in a saucepan, cover with cold water, and add salt and peeled onion.
3. Cook gently until tender, 20 to 30 minutes, with lid on saucepan.
4. Blend the flour with a little of the milk.
5. Drain liquid off tripe, leaving $\frac{2}{3}$ cup in saucepan.
6. Remove the onion, chop, and return to saucepan.
7. Add remaining milk, and butter.
8. When nearly boiling, add blended flour and stir till boiling, then cook for 1 minute.

(continued)

9. Add chopped parsley.
10. Serve on a hot plate.

Note. Rolls of grilled bacon (see p. 18) and sippets of dry toast may be used as a garnish.

ROAST VEAL

1. Prepare oven.
2. Wipe the joint over with a damp cloth.
3. Weigh and allow 40 minutes' cooking time for each 500 g.
4. Season if desired with veal forcemeat (p. 165). Place one tablespoon of fat on joint and one in the dish.
5. Cook in moderate oven, 180°–200°C, for the required time.
6. Cook vegetables with the joint (see p. 36). Allow 40 to 45 minutes.
7. When cooked, serve on a hot plate, and garnish with sliced lemon.

Note. Boiled bacon or pickled pork and thick brown gravy (p. 140) are served with roast veal.

VIENNA SCHNITZEL

500 g fillet of veal
2 lemons
$\frac{1}{4}$ cup flour
$\frac{1}{4}$ teaspoon salt
Pinch pepper
1 egg
$\frac{1}{2}$ cup white breadcrumbs
4 tablespoons melted butter or oil

1. Beat meat slices with a meat mallet until half their original thickness.
2. Pour juice of 1 lemon over meat, and let stand for $\frac{1}{2}$ hour, turning several times.
3. Coat meat with flour, salt, and pepper, then with beaten egg, and roll in breadcrumbs.
4. Melt butter or heat oil, and fry meat gently on each side until cooked—10 to 15 minutes.
5. Drain on absorbent paper.
6. Serve hot, garnished with wedges of the remaining lemon.

VEGETABLES

Vegetables should be cooked in a *small* quantity of boiling water with the lid on the saucepan to prevent loss of nutriment. The quantity of salt varies according to taste. Liquid drained from cooked vegetables may be saved and used for stews or gravies.

Young vegetables may be cooked by the following method: Place prepared vegetables in saucepan with a tablespoon of butter or margarine, salt, and barely enough boiling water to cover base of saucepan. Cook gently with lid on until tender. Shake saucepan occasionally.

Frozen, tinned and dried vegetables: Follow instructions given by the manufacturer.

BAKED VEGETABLES

1. Prepare vegetables according to kind.
2. Dry thoroughly.
3. Put in baking dish with meat and cook for 40 to 45 minutes.
4. Turn once.
5. Drain on absorbent paper.
6. Serve hot, sprinkled with salt and pepper.

ASPARAGUS

1 bunch asparagus
1 teaspoon sugar
Salt
$\frac{1}{2}$ teaspoon vinegar

1. Wash and scrape each stick of asparagus, being careful not to break the tops.
2. Tie into bundles, keeping the tops together.
3. Add sugar, salt, and vinegar.
4. Place asparagus upright in saucepan.
5. Add enough boiling water to reach the base of the green tips.
6. Boil 20 to 30 minutes, or until tender.
7. Remove carefully, drain.
8. Remove the string.
9. Pour melted butter over, and serve hot.

BEANS

500 g beans
Salt
1 teaspoon butter
Pinch pepper

1. Wash beans.
2. Cut off ends and strings from sides.
3. Slice or leave whole as preferred.
4. Place beans in saucepan, add salt, and cover with boiling water.
5. Boil 2 minutes then place on lid, boil till tender—15 to 20 minutes.
6. Drain.
7. Put the butter in the hot saucepan, return beans and pepper, and shake lightly over the heat (do not stir).
8. Serve on a hot dish.

BROAD BEANS

500 g broad beans
Salt
Butter

1. Shell beans and wash.
2. Put beans in a saucepan, add salt, and cover with boiling water.
3. Boil 2 minutes, then put lid on saucepan and boil for a further 10 to 20 minutes until tender.
4. Drain.
5. Place on a hot dish with a little butter.
6. Serve very hot.

BOILED BEETROOT

1. Cut tops off beetroot, leaving 15 cm of the stalks on the roots.
2. Wash thoroughly. Be careful not to scrape or cut.
3. Place beetroot in saucepan and cover with boiling water.
4. Boil with the lid on till tender.
5. Test if cooked (stalk will leave root).
6. Drain.
7. Remove skin.
8. Serve hot as a vegetable or use for pickling (see cold beetroot p. 45).

CABBAGE OR SPINACH

1 cabbage or 1 bunch spinach
Salt
2 tablespoons butter or
    margarine
1 pinch pepper

1. Wash and slice cabbage or spinach.
2. Place just enough boiling water in a saucepan to cover the base.
3. Add salt and butter.
4. Add sliced vegetable.
5. Cover with a tightly fitting lid.
6. Simmer gently 7 to 10 minutes or until tender. Shake saucepan occasionally but do not remove lid.
7. Drain thoroughly, pressing out the water.
8. Serve hot, sprinkled with pepper.

CARROTS OR PARSNIPS

1. Wash well.
2. Scrape if skins are tough. Cut as required.
3. Place in saucepan, add salt, and cover with boiling water.
4. Boil with the lid on until tender, from 15 to 20 minutes.
5. Drain.
6. Serve on a hot dish or plate.

CAULIFLOWER OR BROCCOLI

1. Cut away the thick stalk and outside leaves leaving the green ones that curl into the flowers.
2. Wash well under tap or in salted water.
3. Place in saucepan, add salt, and cover with boiling water.
4. Boil gently with lid on until tender —15 to 20 minutes.
5. Lift out carefully.
6. Place in a hot dish or plate.
7. Serve cauliflower covered with masking sauce (see p. 144); serve broccoli with a little butter and pepper.

CELERY

1. Separate celery, wash well.
2. Cut into pieces about 2 cm long.
3. Place in saucepan, add salt, and cover with the boiling water.
4. Boil gently with the lid on until tender — 15 to 20 minutes.
5. Drain.
6. Place on a hot dish and cover with masking sauce (see p. 144), using celery liquid with milk.

CHOKOES OR JERUSALEM ARTICHOKES

1. Wash well.
2. Peel if required.
3. Cut chokoes into halves or quarters; leave artichokes whole.
4. Place in saucepan, add salt, and cover with boiling water.
5. Boil gently with lid on 20 to 30 minutes or until tender.
6. Drain
7. Serve on a hot dish or plate coated with masking sauce (see p. 144).

GLOBE ARTICHOKES

1. Wash well in salted water.
2. Place in saucepan, add salt, and cover with boiling water.
3. Boil with the lid on tightly until tender — 10 to 15 minutes.
4. Drain.
5. Serve on a hot dish or plate, with a little butter on each and sprinkled with a little pepper.

MARROW, SQUASH, OR ZUCCHINI

1. Wash.
2. Cut into pieces or leave whole, as preferred.
3. Peel thinly unless young.
4. Place in saucepan, add salt, and cover with boiling water.
5. Boil with lid on until tender — 10 to 15 minutes.
6. Lift out carefully or drain.
7. Serve on a hot dish or plate. Cover marrow or squash with masking sauce (see p. 144), and garnish with finely chopped parsley; serve zucchini with butter and pepper.

ONIONS OR LEEKS

1. Remove outer skins and wash.
2. Place in saucepan, add salt, and cover with boiling water.
3. Boil 2 minutes, then put lid on saucepan and boil 20 to 30 minutes or until tender.
4. Drain.
5. Serve on a hot dish or plate with masking sauce (p. 144).

GREEN PEAS

500 g peas
Salt
1 teaspoon sugar
3 sprigs mint
1 teaspoon butter
Pinch pepper

1. Shell peas and wash.
2. Place in saucepan, add salt, sugar, and mint, and cover with boiling water.
3. Boil gently with lid on until tender — 10 to 15 minutes.
4. Drain.
5. Remove mint.
6. Add butter and pepper.
7. Shake over heat.
8. Serve on a hot dish or plate.

BOILED POTATOES

1. Wash, scrub, and dry potatoes.
2. Peel very thinly if necessary, remove the eyes, and cut into pieces of equal size.
3. Put in saucepan, add salt, and cover with boiling water.
4. Boil gently with lid on until tender, about 15 to 20 minutes.
5. Test with a skewer; if soft on the outside and just a little firm in the centre, they are cooked.
6. Drain.
7. Serve whole or mashed (see below).

MASHED POTATOES

4 medium-size boiled potatoes (see above)
2 teaspoons butter
2 tablespoons milk

1. Mash potatoes in the saucepan using potato masher, fork, or wooden spoon.
2. Add butter and milk.
3. Beat well.
4. Stir over stove to reheat.
5. Serve on a hot dish or plate.

POTATO CHIPS

1. Wash, dry, and thinly peel potatoes.
2. Cut into thin strips or fancy shapes.
3. Thoroughly dry.
4. Half fill a saucepan with fat, and heat slowly till a blue fume rises.
5. Place potatoes in a frying basket, lower into fat, and cook 2 to 3 minutes.
6. Lift out and allow fat to become smoking hot.
7. Put chips into fat again, and fry till golden brown.
8. Drain on absorbent paper, sprinkle with pepper and salt, and serve.

SCALLOPED POTATOES

1 teaspoon butter
2 potatoes (medium)
1 onion
1 tablespoon flour
Salt and pepper
Milk
2 tablespoons grated cheese

1. Grease an ovenproof dish with butter.
2. Peel and thinly slice potatoes and onion.
3. Pack in layers in dish, sprinkling each layer with a little flour and salt and pepper.
4. Pour in enough milk to just cover potato and onion.
5. Spread cheese on top.
6. Bake in a moderate oven about 1 hour.

BOILED PUMPKIN

1. Wash well.
2. Cut into pieces and remove the seeds.
3. Place in saucepan, add salt, and cover with boiling water.
4. Boil with lid on for 15 to 20 minutes till tender.
5. Drain.
6. Serve whole, or mashed with butter and pepper, on a hot dish or plate.

SWEET CORN

1. Remove husks.
2. Wash.
3. Place in a saucepan and cover with boiling water (no salt).
4. Boil gently for 8 to 12 minutes until tender.
5. Serve with butter and sprinkle with salt and pepper.

WHITE OR SWEDE TURNIPS

1. Scrub.
2. Peel thickly and cut into suitable sizes.
3. Place in saucepan, add salt, and cover with boiling water.
4. Boil until tender—15 to 20 minutes.
5. Drain.
6. Serve whole, or mashed with a little butter and pepper, on a hot dish or plate.

SALADS AND SALAD DRESSINGS

Preparation of Vegetables for Salad

Cucumber: Wash. Peel or score. Slice thinly.
Celery: Wash. Cut into suitable lengths or chop. To curl celery for garnish, cut into 2 cm to 4 cm lengths, then from one end cut into strips to within 1 cm of the other end, and soak in cold or iced water.
Tomatoes: Wash. Remove skins if preferred. Slice or cut into wedges.
Capsicums: Wash, remove centre and seeds. Cut into rings or dice.
Carrots: Wash. Peel. Grate or slice finely.
Radishes: Wash. Remove roots and leaves. Cut into shapes or leave whole.

Individual or side salads can be prepared by arranging small salads in lettuce leaves.

SALAD

1 lettuce
1 or 2 hard-cooked eggs (see p. 45).
Tomatoes
Cold beetroot (see p. 45)
Any fruit or vegetables in season
$\frac{2}{3}$ cup salad dressing (see p. 45)

1. Remove the coarse outside leaves from the lettuce.
2. Separate lettuce leaves, examining each one carefully on both sides, and wash thoroughly.
3. Allow to drain for a few minutes and then shake lightly in a cloth to dry.
4. Remove the midrib from the larger leaves.
5. Take 3 or 4 leaves at a time, and slice very thinly, or tear into small pieces with the fingers. If preferred, leaves may be left uncut.
6. Place in a glass dish or salad bowl,
7. Garnish tastefully with slices of hard-cooked egg and tomato, beetroot cut into fancy shapes, and any other fruit or vegetables available.

(continued)

8. Serve salad dressing separately in a small jug or bowl.

Note. Salads should be served soon after they are prepared, as they soon become limp.

TOSSED SALAD

Crisp lettuce
Cucumber
Green capsicum
Onion or shallots
Celery
Carrot
Tomato
French dressing (see p. 46).

1. Wash and prepare vegetables.
2. Tear lettuce with fingers.
3. Slice or dice cucumber, capsicum, and onion.
4. Curl celery (see p. 43) and grate carrot.
5. Cut tomato into wedges.
6. Tumble all vegetables in bowl with French dressing.

COLD VEGETABLE SALAD

Cold cooked potatoes, peas, cauliflower, carrots, and beans
Chopped parsley
Chopped shallot
Salad dressing (see p. 45).

1. Cut the cold vegetables into neat dice.
2. Place a layer of the vegetable in a glass dish; sprinkle with a little chopped parsley and shallot.
3. Proceed thus till all the vegetables are used up.
4. Garnish to taste.
5. Serve the salad dressing separately in a small glass jug or bowl.

Note. Cold broad beans alone make a suitable salad if served with a tasty salad dressing.

COLESLAW

Heart of a young cabbage
1 capsicum
1 apple
1 tablespoon chives or 1 onion
Stick celery
Salt and pepper to taste
1 teaspoon sugar
French dressing (see p. 46).

1. Wash and dry cabbage.
2. Shred finely and place in a bowl.
3. Chop or cut other vegetables and fruit finely, and mix with cabbage.
4. Add salt, pepper, and sugar.
5. Pour dressing over vegetables and mix lightly.

Note. Additional ingredients such as pineapple pieces and grated carrot may be added to the above.

Crumbed Fried Cutlets (p. 22) with potatoe chips (p. 41), grilled tomatoes and brussels sprouts.

COLD BEETROOT

$\frac{2}{3}$ cup vinegar
3 cloves
1 blade mace (optional)
2 teaspoons salt
1 tablespoon sugar
6 peppercorns
1 bunch cooked beetroot (see p. 37).

1. Put vinegar, cloves, mace, salt, sugar, and peppercorns in a saucepan.
2. Bring to the boil and simmer 3 minutes.
3. Strain and stand aside until cool.
4. Peel beetroot and slice.
5. Place sliced beetroot in a bowl and pour liquid over it.

HARD-COOKED EGGS FOR SALADS, ETC.

1. Place eggs in boiling water, unless taken from the refrigerator, in which case place in cold water and bring to boil.
2. Allow to simmer gently 15 to 20 minutes.
3. Lift out and stand in a basin of cold water to prevent eggs from discolouring.

SALAD DRESSING (1)

1 yolk hard-cooked egg
$\frac{1}{4}$ teaspoon mustard
2 teaspoons sugar
$\frac{1}{2}$ teaspoon salt
1 teaspoon lucca oil or melted butter
3 tablespoons milk or cream, or 1 tablespoon condensed milk
3 tablespoons vinegar

1. Pound the yolk of the egg in a basin with the back of a wooden spoon.
2. Add mustard, sugar, and salt.
3. Work oil in gradually, very slowly add milk or cream, and vinegar last.
4. Serve in a small glass jug or pour over salad.

Note. When condensed milk is used instead of cream, omit the sugar.

SALAD DRESSING (2)

$\frac{1}{4}$ teaspoon mustard
$\frac{1}{2}$ teaspoon salt
2 teaspoons sugar
1 tablespoon condensed milk
2 tablespoons milk
2 tablespoons vinegar

1. Mix mustard, salt, sugar, and condensed milk together in a small basin.
2. Add milk.
3. Stir in vinegar last, very gradually.
4. Serve in a small jug or pour onto salad.

Goulash (p. 23) with boiled rice (p. 5) and coleslaw (p. 44).

COOKED SALAD DRESSING

2 tablespoons butter
1 egg
$\frac{1}{2}$ cup milk
$\frac{1}{2}$ cup sugar
$\frac{1}{2}$ teaspoon salt
1 teaspoon mustard
$\frac{1}{4}$ cup vinegar

1. Melt butter in a saucepan; remove from heat.
2. Add beaten egg and milk.
3. Add sugar, salt, and mustard.
4. Add vinegar last.
5. Return to heat and stir till it coats the spoon, without boiling.

Note. This is better made in a double saucepan. It will keep for three weeks if chilled.

FRENCH DRESSING

2 tablespoons oil
2 tablespoons vinegar
Salt and cayenne to taste

1. Place oil in a container.
2. Add vinegar drop by drop, beating and shaking vigorously till smooth.
3. Season.

MAYONNAISE

2 egg yolks (raw)
$\frac{1}{2}$ teaspoon salt
Pinch pepper
$\frac{1}{4}$ teaspoon mustard
6 tablespoons lucca oil or melted butter
2 tablespoons tarragon vinegar

1. Place egg yolks, salt, pepper, and mustard in a basin; mix well.
2. Add a few drops of oil or butter and work in very gradually with a wooden spoon.
3. Add a few drops of vinegar and work in very gradually.
4. Continue very slowly till all the oil and vinegar are added.

Note. The success of this recipe depends on the continuous beating, and on making the mayonnaise in a very cool place; in warm weather it is best to place the basin on ice while beating.

COLD MEAT COOKERY

COLD MEAT FRITTERS

6 slices cold meat
A little lemon juice
Pinch pepper
1 quantity fritter batter (see p. 88)
1 teaspoon salt
1 tablespoon chopped parsley
Frying fat

1. Lay the slices of meat on a plate.
2. Sprinkle with the lemon juice and pepper.
3. Let stand half an hour.
4. Make the batter and add the salt and chopped parsley.
5. Dip each piece of meat into batter, using a spoon.
6. Fry in a deep frying-pan with a large quantity of hot fat.
7. Lift out with a spoon or drainer.
8. Drain on absorbent paper.
9. Serve on a hot plate and garnish with sprigs of parsley.

CURRY AND RICE

250 g cooked meat
1 apple
1 onion
1 tablespoon fat
1 tablespoon sultanas
1 teaspoon salt
1 pinch pepper
1 tablespoon sugar
2 teaspoons curry powder
1 tablespoon plain flour
1 cup stock or water
1 teaspoon lemon juice
$\frac{1}{2}$ cup rice (boiled) (see p. 5)

1. Cut meat into small pieces, removing all fat and gristle.
2. Cut apple and onion into dice.
3. Heat fat in a saucepan.
4. Fry the onion and apple.
5. Add all the dry ingredients except meat and rice, and stir for one minute over heat.
6. Add water or stock and stir till boiling.
7. Simmer gently for 15 minutes.
8. Add the meat and lemon juice and allow to simmer in the sauce till meat is thoroughly heated, about 10 minutes.
9. Serve on a hot plate, and arrange rice round the curry and garnish with thin half slices of lemon, standing the lemon up.
10. Grate the yolk of a hard-cooked egg over the rice, or sprinkle with chopped parsley.

MEAT LOAF

500 g (1¾ cups) hamburger mince
50 g (¾ cup) sausage mince
2 bacon rashers
1 cup fresh breadcrumbs
½ teaspoon salt
½ teaspoon pepper
1 egg
1 tablespoon tomato sauce
1 tablespoon Worcestershire sauce
3 hard-cooked eggs

1. Grease loaf pan.
2. Place mince in basin.
3. Chop bacon finely; add to breadcrumbs salt, and pepper, and mix with mince.
4. Beat egg, add sauces, and mix well with other ingredients.
5. Put half the mixture into prepared pan.
6. Place the hard-cooked eggs down the centre lengthwise, and cover with the other half of mince mixture.
7. Bake in moderate over, $180°-190°C$, about 1½ hours.

Note. The pan may be covered with greaseproof paper or foil for 1 hour, after which the paper or foil is removed to allow the meat to brown.

RISSOLES OF COLD MEAT

125 g cooked meat
2 tablespoons flour
1 tablespoon fresh bread-crumbs
1 tablespoon chopped parsley
½ teaspoon herbs
Pinch pepper
¼ teaspoon salt
⅔ cup stock or water
Seasoned flour, egg glazing, 1 cup breadcrumbs

1. Chop or mince the meat finely, removing skin and gristle.
2. Place in a saucepan with the flour, 1 tablespoon breadcrumbs, parsley, herbs, pepper, salt, and water.
3. Stir over heat till it becomes thick.
4. Turn onto a plate to cool.
5. Beat the egg slightly on a plate.
6. Spread the cup of breadcrumbs on a sheet of unprinted paper.
7. Sprinkle a little flour on a board.
8. Take tablespoons of the mixture and lightly roll in the flour into round or cork shapes, using 2 knives.
9. Brush each rissole over with egg glazing.
10. Roll in the crumbs.
11. Press crumbs on firmly with a knife.
12. Fry a golden brown colour in hot fat.
13. Drain on absorbent paper.
14. Serve on a hot plate, and garnish with sprigs of parsley.

SHEPHERD'S PIE

250 g cooked meat
$\frac{1}{4}$ teaspoon chopped herbs
1 tablespoon chopped parsley
1 tablespoon plain flour
$\frac{1}{4}$ teaspoon salt
Pinch pepper
A little grated lemon rind or
    nutmeg (optional)
$\frac{1}{2}$ cup stock or water
4 medium-size cold cooked
    potatoes
A little butter and milk

1. Chop the meat finely, removing skin and gristle.
2. Put in a saucepan with herbs, parsley, flour, salt, pepper, lemon rind or nutmeg, and stock or water, and stir over heat for 5 minutes or till it leaves the side of the saucepan.
3. Mash the potatoes, adding a little butter and milk to make them smooth.
4. Grease a pie-dish.
5. Line pie-dish with a thin layer of mashed potato.
6. Add the meat mixture.
7. Cover with remaining potato, smoothing the top with a broad knife dipped in milk.
8. Score into squares and mark the edge with a fork.
9. Put pie into a moderate oven, $180°-190°$ C, to re-heat till a pale brown colour.
10. Serve garnished with parsley.

STUFFED TOMATOES

4 large tomatoes
1 cup finely chopped cold
    meat or 2 finely chop-
    ped hard-cooked eggs
    or 3 tablespoons grated
    cheese
4 tablespoons fresh bread-
    crumbs
1 tablespoon chopped parsley
A little grated nutmeg
Pinch pepper
1 teaspoon salt
1 tablespoon butter

1. Cut the tops off the tomatoes and scoop out the inside.
2. Sprinkle with a little salt and pepper.
3. Mix the meat or egg or grated cheese with 1 tablespoon breadcrumbs, parsley, nutmeg, pepper, salt, and 2 tablespoons of tomato pulp.
4. Fill the tomatoes with the mixture.
5. Sprinkle the remainder of the crumbs on the top.
6. Place a small piece of butter on each.
7. Replace the tops on the tomatoes.
8. Bake in a moderate oven, $180°-190°$ C, for 15 to 20 minutes.
9. Serve on slices of toast or fried bread and garnish with small sprigs of parsley.

TO RE-HEAT COLD ROAST BEEF

1. Cut beef into slices.
2. Bring gravy to boiling point.
3. Reduce the heat and place the slices in, simmer just long enough to heat right through.

SAVOURY DISHES

These can be made from a wide variety of foods and provide suitable dishes for luncheons, teas, and suppers.

BEAN AND ONION CASSEROLE

1 small onion
1 tablespoon margarine
Salt and pepper to taste
$\frac{1}{2}$ teaspoon curry powder
1 small apple
1 carrot
1 tomato
$\frac{1}{2}$ cup cooked soya or haricot beans
$\frac{1}{4}$ cup stock or water (if needed)
1 tablespoon grated cheese
1 tablespoon breadcrumbs

1. Fry onion in margarine.
2. Add salt, pepper, and curry. Cook one minute.
3. Add diced apple and carrot, sliced tomato, and cooked beans.
4. Cook 10 minutes, stirring all the time.
5. Add stock if needed.
6. Place in greased casserole.
7. Sprinkle with cheese and breadcrumbs.
8. Brown in 180°C oven 15 to 20 minutes.

To cook dried beans
1. Soak overnight, well covered with warm water containing $\frac{1}{8}$ teaspoon bicarbonate of soda.
2. Boil water in which beans have soaked. Add salt to taste.
3. Add beans and cook gently with lid on saucepan till tender. Add extra boiling water while cooking if necessary.

Note. The use of a pressure cooker will reduce cooking time.

STUFFED CAPSICUMS

3 capsicums
1 tablespoon margarine
1 tablespoon plain flour
$\frac{1}{2}$ cup milk
Salt and pepper to taste

1. Wash capsicums.
2. Remove stalk ends and seeds.
3. Parboil gently in boiling salted water for 10 minutes.
4. Drain.

(continued)

1 teaspoon tomato sauce
1 cup cold minced meat
1 small can whole corn
3 tablespoons dried bread-
    crumbs
Stock or water (about 1 cup)

5. Melt margarine in saucepan, add flour, and
    mix well; cook 1 minute.
6. Add milk and stir until boiling.
7. Combine this sauce with salt, pepper, tomato
    sauce, meat, and well-drained corn.
8. Fill the capsicums and sprinkle with bread-
    crumbs.
9. Place into a greased ovenproof dish with stock
    or water.
10. Bake in a moderate oven 180°–200°C, until
    tender, about 15 minutes.

CAULIFLOWER AU GRATIN

1 cauliflower (cooked)
1 cup melted butter masking
    sauce (see p. 144).
$\frac{1}{2}$ cup grated cheese
1 tablespoon dried bread-
    crumbs
1 tablespoon butter

1. Place cauliflower in an ovenproof dish.
2. Mask with masking sauce.
3. Sprinkle with grated cheese and breadcrumbs.
4. Put butter in small pieces on top.
5. Bake in a moderately hot oven, 180°–200°C,
    until a golden brown—10 to 15 minutes.

Note. Carrots, marrow, and other suitable vegetables may be done in the same way.

CELERY AND SPAGHETTI AU GRATIN

2 cups diced cooked celery
1 cup cooked spaghetti
1 cup melted butter masking
    sauce (see p. 144)
1 cup grated cheese
$\frac{1}{2}$ cup fresh breadcrumbs
2 teaspoons butter

1. Mix celery and spaghetti.
2. Stir in masking sauce and grated cheese. Mix
    well.
3. Turn into a greased ovenproof dish.
4. Cover with breadcrumbs.
5. Dot small pieces of butter over the top.
6. Bake in moderate oven, 180°–200°C, for 30
    to 40 minutes.

CHEESE BALLS

$\frac{1}{4}$ cup plain flour
Pinch salt and cayenne
$\frac{1}{2}$ cup grated cheese
1 egg
Squeeze lemon juice

1. Sift flour, salt, and cayenne.
2. Mix cheese with flour.
3. Separate yolk from white of egg.
4. Beat yolk and lemon juice together and mix
    with dry ingredients.

(continued)

Frying fat

5. Add stiffly beaten white of egg.
6. Heat fat in frying-pan.
7. Drop in small portions of mixture.
8. Fry light brown.
9. Drain on absorbent paper.
10. Serve hot, sprinkled with grated cheese.

BAKED CHEESE CUSTARD

3 eggs
½ cup soft white breadcrumbs
1 cup milk
¼ teaspoon salt
½ teaspoon mustard
½ cup grated cheese

1. Beat egg whites until stiff.
2. To the slightly beaten egg yolks add bread-crumbs, milk, salt, mustard, and cheese.
3. Fold in egg whites.
4. Turn into a buttered, uncovered ovenproof dish.
5. Bake in a slow oven, 150°–180°C, for 30 to 40 minutes or until a knife inserted in the centre comes out clean.
6. Serve hot, or cold with salad.

CHEESE SOUFFLÉ

3 tablespoons butter or mar-garine
3 tablespoons plain flour
¼ teaspoon salt
Pinch cayenne pepper
1 cup milk
1 cup grated dry cheese
3 eggs

1. Melt butter in saucepan.
2. Add flour, salt, and cayenne; stir well.
3. Add milk and stir over slow heat until thick.
4. Add cheese and stir till just melted.
5. Separate whites from yolks of eggs.
6. Stir the sauce mixture into the yolks and allow to cool.
7. Beat egg whites in a bowl until stiff.
8. Fold gently into the cheese mixture.
9. Place into a well-greased fireproof dish with mixture at least 2 cm from the top of the dish.
10. Bake in a slow oven, 150°–180°C, for 30 to 40 minutes.
11. Serve at once on heated plates.

SALMON SOUFFLÉ

Use recipe as above, substituting a small can of well-drained flaked salmon, with one teaspoon of lemon juice, for the cheese.

CHEESE SOUFFLÉ TARTS

1 quantity shortcrust pastry
    (see p. 93)
2 eggs
½ cup grated cheese
Salt and cayenne pepper to
    taste
1 teaspoon chopped parsley

1. Roll pastry, and line patty pans with cut-out pastry shapes.
2. Separate whites from yolks of eggs.
3. Add cheese, seasonings, and parsley to yolks. Mix well.
4. Beat whites until stiff and fold into other ingredients.
5. Spoon into pastry cases.
6. Bake at 200°–230°C for 10 to 15 minutes.

CHEESE AND VEGETABLE BAKE

3 large ripe tomatoes
2 large white onions
2 or 3 bacon rashers
1 cup fresh breadcrumbs
2 cups grated cheese
Pepper and salt to taste
1 teaspoon dry mustard
2 cups mashed potatoes
Milk for glazing

1. Peel tomatoes and slice thickly.
2. Peel onions and slice thinly.
3. Remove rind and chop bacon finely.
4. Grease an ovenproof dish.
5. Fill with alternate layers of tomatoes, breadcrumbs, onion, cheese, and bacon.
6. Sprinkle each layer with salt, pepper, and mustard.
7. Spread potato on top.
8. Glaze with milk.
9. Bake in a moderate oven, 180°–200°C, for about 40 minutes.

CHEESE AND VEGETABLE PIE

1 stick celery
1 small onion
½ turnip
1 small carrot
½ cup shelled peas
1¼ cups of melted butter sauce
    No. 3 (see p. 144)
Double quantity shortcrust
    pastry (see p. 93)
½ cup grated cheese
Milk for glazing

1. Prepare vegetables and cut into dice.
2. Cook vegetables until tender (any left over cold vegetables could be used).
3. Combine vegetables with sauce.
4. Cut pastry in halves.
5. Roll one portion and line a 20 cm pie plate.
6. Fill with vegetable mixture.
7. Sprinkle with cheese.
8. Roll out the remaining pastry and cover the mixture, pressing edges firmly.
9. Glaze with milk.

(continued)

10. Bake in a hot oven, 220°–230°C, for about 20 minutes.

Note. Mashed potato may be used instead of pastry to make this dish.

CHICKEN AND ALMONDS

¼ cup blanched almonds
2 tablespoons melted butter or fat
1 small roasting chicken (approximately 1 kg)
125 g fresh mushrooms *or* one 125 g can of mushrooms
1 tablespoon maize cornflour
½ teaspoon salt
1 tablespoon soy sauce
1 small onion, diced
1 clove garlic, crushed (optional)
2 cups diced celery
3 shallots cut in 2.5 cm pieces
1 cup chicken stock or water

1. Fry almonds in 1 tablespoon of butter or fat until golden brown.
2. Drain almonds and set aside. Return fat to pan.
3. Remove chicken flesh from bones and cut into dice.
4. Skin and dice the mushrooms if using fresh ones, and chop onion.
5. Coat chicken pieces with the cornflour and salt, then sprinkle with soy sauce.
6. Add second tablespoon of butter or fat to the pan and fry the onion (and garlic, if used) until limp but not brown.
7. Add chicken pieces and cook over low heat, stirring briskly. The chicken flesh should change colour but must not brown. The time will vary according to the size of the pieces and the area of the pan, so test a small piece for tenderness.
8. Add mushrooms and celery. Cook 8 to 10 minutes, stirring constantly. Add almonds and shallots.
9. Add stock and stir until boiling. Taste and adjust salt if desired.
10. Serve hot with fried rice.

CHICKEN CASSEROLE

1 capsicum
4 tomatoes
2 small onions
2 tablespoons butter or margarine
2 tablespoons plain flour

1. Prepare vegetables (peel tomatoes) and slice.
2. Melt butter or margarine.
3. Add flour; cook 1 minute.
4. Add apricot nectar all at once; stir until it thickens.
5. Add onion, capsicum, salt and pepper, and

(continued)

1½ cups of apricot nectar
Salt and pepper to taste
1 steamed chicken
2 tablespoons dried breadcrumbs
½ tablespoon chopped parsley

simmer until the vegetables are tender.
6. Cut chicken into small pieces and place in casserole dish.
7. Add sliced tomatoes, cover with sauce, and sprinkle with breadcrumbs and parsley.
8. Reheat in oven.

CHICKEN CREAM

1 medium-sized chicken, previously steamed or pressure cooked
125 g mushrooms
1 small red capsicum
1 small green capsicum
3 tablespoons butter or margarine
3 tablespoons plain flour
1¼ cups milk
2 egg yolks
Salt and pepper to taste
Toast slices or pastry cases

1. Cut chicken into small pieces, discarding skin and bone.
2. Slice mushrooms and capsicums and fry in 1 tablespoon of the butter or margarine until limp but not brown.
3. Remove mushrooms and capsicums from pan and set aside; leave butter or margarine in pan.
4. Add the remaining butter or margarine and stir over low heat until just melted.
5. Mix in flour until smooth, then blend in the milk.
6. Stir over moderate heat until it boils and thickens.
7. Mix egg yolks in a small basin with 1 table-spoon of the hot sauce.
8. Stir egg mixture into remaining sauce, then add the chicken and vegetables. Taste and add salt and pepper as desired.
9. Stir over moderate heat until thoroughly hot but not boiling.
10. Serve hot with triangles of toast or in ready-made puff pastry cases.

Note. Serves 4 as a dinner, or would fill 2 dozen small pastry cases for a party.

CORN FRITTERS

1 small can sweet corn (whole kernel)
1 quantity fritter batter (see p. 88)
Frying fat

1. Pour the liquid off corn and put corn into batter. Mix well.
2. Put a spoonful of the mixture into a saucepan of hot fat and fry until a golden brown.

(continued)

3. Lift out with a slice or iron spoon and drain on absorbent paper.
4. Serve on a hot dish or plate, and garnish with sprigs of parsley.

EGG AND BACON PIE

250 g shortcrust or flaky
    pastry (see pp. 93, 92)
3-4 rashers bacon
4 eggs
1¼ cups milk
¼ teaspoon salt
Pepper to taste
1 tablespoon chopped parsley

1. Line 20 cm pie plate with half the pastry.
2. Remove rind and chop bacon; sprinkle in pie plate.
3. Beat eggs with milk, and add seasoning and parsley.
4. Pour over bacon.
5. Glaze edge of pastry and roll remaining pastry to fit top.
6. Press the edges together and cut a slit in the middle of the pie.
7. Glaze the pastry and decorate.
8. Bake at 230°C for 10 minutes; reduce heat to 180°C and cook a further 20 to 25 minutes.

CURRIED EGGS

½ cup rice
3 tablespoons butter
2 teaspoons curry powder
3 tablespoons plain flour
¼ teaspoon salt
1¼ cups milk
Squeeze lemon juice
4 hard-cooked eggs

1. Boil rice according to recipe on page 5.
2. Make butter hot in saucepan.
3. Add curry powder, flour, and salt, and stir for 1 minute.
4. Add milk, stir till boiling, and cook 3 minutes, add lemon juice.
5. Shell the eggs, cut lengthwise into quarters, put into curry sauce and stand at side of heat for ¼ hour; it must not boil.
6. Serve on a hot dish or plate with a border of boiled rice, and garnish with slices of lemon and finely chopped parsley.

FISH KEDGEREE

250 g cold cooked fish
Parsley
2 hard-cooked eggs

1. Skin, bone, and flake fish. Chop parsley.
2. Remove yolks from eggs; chop whites.
3. Boil rice till tender; drain and reheat.

(continued)

¼ cup rice
1 tablespoon butter
Salt and pepper
Lemon juice
¼ cup milk

4. Melt butter in saucepan.
5. Add chopped egg white, fish, chopped parsley, salt and pepper, lemon juice, and milk. Heat well.
6. Arrange heated rice on hot dish.
7. Place fish on top of rice, making into a pyramid.
8. Rub egg yolks through strainer and sprinkle over fish.
9. Garnish with lemon and sprigs of parsley.

FISH MORNAY

½ teaspoon lemon juice
Salt and cayenne to taste
125 g salmon or tuna or scallops or oysters or cooked fish
1¼ cups melted butter masking sauce (see p. 144)
1 tablespoon grated cheese
1 tablespoon dried breadcrumbs

1. Add lemon juice, salt, cayenne, and fish to sauce.
2. Grease fireproof dish.
3. Place mixture into greased dish.
4. Sprinkle cheese and breadcrumbs on top.
5. Brown lightly in oven or under griller.
6. Serve garnished with parsley or lemon wedges.

CHICKEN MORNAY

Use recipe as above substituting cooked chicken for fish.

EGG MORNAY

Use recipe as above substituting hard-cooked eggs cut into wedges for fish.

KIDNEY AND BACON

1 small onion
⅔ cup water
½ rasher bacon
1 sheep's kidney
2 teaspoons plain flour
Salt to taste

1. Dice or grate onion. Boil water.
2. Place onion in boiling water; simmer gently until tender.
3. Remove rind from bacon. Cut bacon into small pieces.

(continued)

4. Remove skin and core from kidney. Wash well.
5. Slice kidney finely.
6. Add kidney and bacon to onion.
7. Simmer gently 6 minutes or until tender.
8. Blend flour and salt with a little extra water. Add to kidney and stir till it comes to the boil and thickens.
9. Serve on a hot plate and sprinkle with finely chopped parsley.

LENTIL AND EGG CURRY

1 cup dried lentils
2 medium-size onions
3 tablespoons butter
1 tablespoon curry powder
$\frac{3}{4}$ cup water
4 hard-cooked eggs
$\frac{1}{2}$ teaspoon salt

1. Soak lentils overnight.
2. Peel and slice onions.
3. Melt butter in saucepan. Add onions and curry powder.
4. Cook slowly 10 minutes, stirring frequently.
5. Add water and lentils.
6. Cover and cook gently over low heat for 45 minutes or until lentils are tender.
7. Slice eggs and add with salt to the lentil mixture.
8. Mix gently and cook slowly for 5 minutes.
9. Serve hot.

MACARONI CHEESE

60 g macaroni
2 tablespoons butter
2 tablespoons plain flour
$1\frac{1}{4}$ cups milk
1 teaspoon mustard
$\frac{1}{2}$ teaspoon salt
Pinch cayenne pepper
$\frac{1}{2}$ cup grated cheese

1. Have ready a saucepan of boiling salted water.
2. Break macaroni into 2 cm pieces and wash well.
3. Drop macaroni into boiling water; boil for 25 minutes, or until tender, with lid off the saucepan.
4. Drain.
5. Melt butter in saucepan.
6. Add flour off the heat; mix thoroughly, and cook gently 1 minute (it must not be allowed to brown).
7. Add milk; stir until boiling.
8. Season with mustard, salt, and cayenne pepper.

(continued)

9. Add macaroni and half the cheese to sauce.
10. Pour into a greased pie-dish.
11. Sprinkle remainder of cheese on top; put a few pieces of butter round the edge of dish.
12. Brown in a hot oven or under a hot griller.

CASSEROLED MEAT BALLS

125 g ($\frac{1}{2}$ cup) minced steak
60 g ($\frac{1}{4}$ cup) sausage mince
1 tablespoon finely minced onion
Salt and pepper to taste
1 tablespoon plain flour
$\frac{1}{2}$ tablespoon gravy powder
$\frac{2}{3}$ cup water
1 tablespoon tomato sauce
$\frac{1}{2}$ tablespoon Worcestershire sauce
1 medium sliced potato

1. Mix meats, onion, salt, and pepper.
2. Shape into balls, roll in flour mixed with gravy powder.
3. Place in greased casserole.
4. Mix water with sauces and pour over meat balls.
5. Peel and slice potato; place in casserole.
6. Cook with lid on 35 to 40 minutes in moderate oven, 180°–200°C.

MINCE AND CHEESEBURGERS

1 kg ($3\frac{1}{2}$ cups) minced steak
$\frac{1}{2}$ teaspoon salt
Pinch pepper
2 onions finely grated
1 cup fresh breadcrumbs
Bread rolls
Cheese slices
Tomato slices

1. Mould the meat, salt, pepper, onion, and breadcrumbs well together into 12 or more thin shapes to fit bread roll.
2. Fry or grill the mixture for 5 to 10 minutes.
3. Place on bread roll with cheese and tomato slices.
4. Serve with salad.

SWEET AND SOUR PORK

1 kg lean pork
2 tablespoons margarine or butter
1 cup sliced carrots
1 cup chopped celery
2 large chopped onions
Pepper
1 teaspoon salt

1. Cut pork into 4 cm pieces, and fry in margarine or butter until meat changes colour.
2. Add carrots, celery, onions, pepper, and salt.
3. Stir in stock and pineapple juice, cover the pan and cook until pork is tender (approximately $1\frac{1}{2}$ hours).
4. Blend the cornflour with the vinegar, water, soy sauce, sugar, and Parisian essence.

(continued)

Steak and Kidney Pie (p. 32) with green peas (p. 40).

1½ cups stock or water
¾ cup pineapple juice
4 tablespoons maize corn-
    flour
1 tablespoon vinegar
1 tablespoon water
1 tablespoon soy sauce
4 tablespoons sugar
Parisian essence
1 small can pineapple pieces
Pepper

5. Stir into pork and vegetable mixture.
6. Add pineapple pieces.
7. Cook over a slow heat until mixture boils.
8. Serve hot with fried or boiled rice.

NUT ROAST

1 small onion
4 medium tomatoes
¾ cup ground nuts
½ teaspoon salt
Pinch pepper
Chopped parsley
2 tablespoons fat
1 teaspoon vegetable extract
5 tablespoons water
1 egg
2 cups cooked mashed po-
    tatoes
2 tablespoons melted short-
    ening
1 cup brown gravy (see p.
    140

1. Peel and dice onion and tomatoes.
2. Fry onion in fat until lightly browned.
3. Combine with all other ingredients except
    gravy and shortening.
4. Press into prepared tin.
5. Bake at 160°–190° C about 1 hour. Baste with
    melted shortening during cooking.
6. Serve with heated brown gravy.

POTATO CAKES AND BACON

2 medium-size boiled po-
    tatoes
1 cup plain flour
¼ teaspoon baking powder
Salt and pepper to taste
1 tablespoon butter
1 egg
1 tablespoon milk
3–4 rashers bacon, fried

1. Mash potatoes.
2. Sift flour with baking powder, pepper, and
    salt.
3. Rub in the butter.
4. Add mashed potatoes.
5. Add beaten egg and milk.
6. Knead on floured board.
7. Roll out 2 cm thick, and cut into neat shapes.
8. Dry fry for 6 minutes. Drain.
9. Serve with fried bacon on a hot dish or plate,
    and garnish with parsley.

Chicken Casserole (p. 55).

POTATO PUFFS

6 medium-size old potatoes
2 teaspoons butter
1 tablespoon milk
1 egg
Salt and pepper to taste

1. Wash, dry and bake potatoes in jackets.
2. Cut potatoes in halves.
3. Remove inside of potato, being careful not to break skin.
4. Mash the removed potato, adding butter, milk, egg yolk, salt, and pepper.
5. Stiffly beat white of egg and mix in lightly.
6. Fill potato cases.
7. Stand in a baking dish and place in a hot oven, $220°-250°C$, for 10 minutes to brown.
8. Serve on a hot dish or plate, garnished with sprigs of parsley.

Note. Finely chopped cold meat or grated cheese may be added to the mixture.

FRIED RICE

3 tablespoons butter
1 cup rice
1 cup finely diced celery
3 stock cubes or chicken noodle soup to make 3 cups of stock
Salt and pepper to taste
1 cup diced onion or shallots
1 cup finely diced capsicum
250 g bacon or ham
3 eggs

1. Heat butter in heavy pan and add dry rice and celery.
2. Cook quickly, stirring all the time, until a golden brown colour.
3. Add stock and salt and pepper. Bring to boil and simmer, with pan covered, until stock has been absorbed; stir occasionally.
4. Prepare onion and capsicum; remove rind and cut bacon into dice.
5. In another pan fry bacon, then onions in bacon fat. Stir in capsicum and heat through.
6. Lightly beat eggs, fry until set and cut into small strips.
7. When rice is cooked fold in all other ingredients. Allow to reheat and serve.

SALMON AND MACARONI

1½ cups macaroni
1 onion
1 can (250 g) salmon or tuna
2 tablespoons butter or margarine

1. Boil the macaroni and diced onion in salted water until tender.
2. Drain well and mix with fish.
3. Place in greased casserole.

(continued)

2 tablespoons flour
2 cups milk
1 sliced tomato
1 tablespoon grated cheese or
    cheese spread

4. Melt butter or margarine.
5. Stir in flour.
6. Add milk and stir till boiling.
7. Pour sauce over fish and macaroni.
8. Top with sliced tomato and cheese.
9. Bake in a moderate oven, 180°–200°C, until brown—about 10 minutes.

Note. Cooked cape cod or smoked haddock can be substituted for the salmon.

SPAGHETTI BOLOGNAISE

500 g (1$\frac{3}{4}$ cups) round steak,
    minced
2 cups tomato puree
3 tablespoons butter or oil
1 small onion, grated or
    chopped finely
3 thin slices of garlic
$\frac{1}{2}$ teaspoon salt
Pepper to taste
$\frac{1}{4}$ teaspoon mixed herbs
1 teaspoon sugar
250 g spaghetti
2 cups boiling water
1 teaspoon salt
2 tablespoons Parmesan
    cheese

1. Place meat, tomato puree, butter, onion, garlic, and seasonings in saucepan.
2. Bring to boil and simmer gently 1$\frac{1}{2}$ hours.
3. Twenty minutes before serving cook the spaghetti: place into boiling salted water, boil gently till tender.
4. Spread the spaghetti on a large serving dish, cover with the meat mixture.
5. Sprinkle with Parmesan cheese, and garnish with sprigs of parsley.

SAVOURY DIPS

Cheese Dip

125 g cream cheese
$\frac{1}{2}$ cup cream
1 tablespoon tomato sauce
1 tablespoon chutney
1 tablespoon Worcestershire
    sauce
1 tablespoon finely chopped
    onion
1 tablespoon finely chopped
    capsicum
1 cup grated tasty cheese

1. Put all ingredients except grated cheese in basin. Mix well.
2. Fold in grated cheese.

Asparagus and Ham Dip

1 small can asparagus cuts
60 g ham
1 hard-cooked egg
½ cup melted butter masking
    sauce (see p. 144)
Salt and pepper to taste

1. Drain asparagus.
2. Finely dice ham and chop egg.
3. Add these ingredients to masking sauce. Mix evenly, adding salt and pepper to taste.

Note. This can also be served on hot, buttered toast.

SPAGHETTI AND MINCE

1 small onion
500 g (1¾ cups) minced steak
Pinch thyme
1¼ cups water
Salt and pepper to taste
125 g spaghetti
2 tablespoons tomato sauce
1 tablespoon cornflour or
    gravy powder
½ cup grated cheese

1. Peel and chop onion.
2. Simmer mince, onion, and thyme with water, salt and pepper for 20 minutes, stirring occasionally.
3. Boil spaghetti in water for 15 minutes, strain, and add to mince with tomato sauce.
4. Thicken with blended cornflour or gravy powder and stir until boiling.
5. Pour into casserole dish and sprinkle with grated cheese.
6. Brown lightly under griller.

STEAK AND PINEAPPLE CASSEROLE

1 small can pineapple pieces
2 tablespoons plain flour
½ teaspoon salt
Pinch pepper
Pinch mixed spice
1 teaspoon mustard
750 g topside or round steak
1 onion
1 tablespoon fat
2 tablespoons vinegar
1 tablespoon soy sauce

1. Drain juice from pineapple pieces and keep aside.
2. Combine flour, salt, pepper, spice, and mustard.
3. Cut meat into pieces, roll in seasoned flour.
4. Peel and chop onion.
5. Melt fat in pan. Brown the onion and place in casserole dish.
6. Brown meat; add pineapple pieces.
7. Mix pineapple juice with sauce and vinegar.
8. Put meat and pineapple pieces into casserole dish.
9. Add juice and sauces. Mix well.
10. Place lid on and cook in a moderate oven, 180°–200°C, for 2 hours or until meat is tender.

TOMATO AND VEGETABLE MINCE

1 cup diced celery
1 cup diced carrot
$\frac{1}{2}$ cup peas
750 g cooked minced steak
2 tomatoes
1 cup cooked rice
1 can (500 g) tomato soup
$\frac{1}{2}$ cup grated cheese
1 small packet potato chips or
$\frac{1}{2}$ cup dried breadcrumbs

1. Cook celery, carrots, and peas until tender.
2. Grease fireproof dish.
3. Place half mince in dish, and cover with half the vegetables.
4. Cover with sliced tomato and half the rice.
5. Pour over half the tomato soup.
6. Repeat layers.
7. Sprinkle with grated cheese and chips or breadcrumbs.
8. Bake at $180°-200°$C till heated right through and browned on top—30 to 40 minutes.

VEGETABLE RICE

$\frac{1}{2}$ green capsicum
1 medium onion
125 g mushrooms
1 carrot
Small wedge cabbage
2 cups cold cooked rice
3 tablespoons oil or melted butter
$\frac{1}{2}$ teaspoon salt
1 dessertspoon sugar
Pinch pepper
2 eggs
1 tablespoon chopped parsley

1. Slice capsicum, onion, and mushrooms thinly.
2. Coarsely grate carrot. Shred cabbage.
3. Fry rice lightly in oil or butter, add prepared vegetables and seasonings, mix well, cover pan, and cook gently 10 minutes. Reduce heat.
4. Beat eggs, make hollow in centre of rice and vegetable mixture, and pour eggs into pan. Leave until half set and then stir through mixture.
5. Serve with chopped parsley.

WELSH RAREBIT

125 g cheese
1 tablespoon butter
1 teaspoon mustard
Cayenne
2 tablespoons milk or cream
2 teaspoons Worcestershire sauce
4 slices buttered toast

1. Slice cheese thinly and mix together with butter, mustard, cayenne, milk, and sauce.
2. Spread on toast.
3. Place under griller or in top of oven for 3 to 4 minutes.
4. Serve very hot.

MILK PUDDINGS

ANGEL'S FOOD

1 egg (60 g)
1 cup milk
2 tablespoons sugar
3 teaspoons gelatine
2 tablespoons hot water
5 drops vanilla essence

1. Separate white from yolk of egg.
2. Heat milk and sugar, pour onto egg yolk, and mix well.
3. Return to saucepan, heat gently, stirring well without boiling, until mixture coats the spoon.
4. Cool.
5. Dissolve gelatine in hot water. Add to cool custard mixture with vanilla.
6. Beat egg white stiffly and fold lightly into mixture.
7. Pour into wet mould and set.
8. Turn out onto a serving dish.

SPANISH CREAM

Recipe as for Angel's Food, but add dissolved gelatine to the hot custard mixture; this allows a jelly to set at the base of the cream mixture.

Note. To add variety, flavour the milk before making the custard:
Add 1 teaspoon of cocoa for chocolate flavour.
Add 1 teaspoon of instant coffee for coffee flavour.
Add 1 tablespoon of caramel sauce and substitute brown sugar for white for caramel flavour.

BLANCMANGE

2 tablespoons maize corn-
    flour
1¼ cups milk
1 tablespoon sugar
Lemon rind or bay leaf or
    peach leaf
3 drops essence (optional)

1. Rinse a mould or small basin with cold water.
2. Blend the cornflour with some of the milk.
3. Put the remainder of the milk on to boil in a small saucepan with sugar and bay leaf or lemon rind or peach leaf.
4. When nearly boiling, remove from stove, lift out leaf or rind, and stir in the blended cornflour.
5. Stir well, return to stove, and cook for 3 minutes after it comes to the boil.
6. Add the essence if required.
7. Pour into the wet mould.
8. Stand mould in a shallow basin of cold water to set. Chill.
9. When quite cold. loosen round edge, and turn it out into a serving dish.
10. Serve with jam, stewed fruit, or custard.

BAKED CUSTARD

1 egg
1 tablespoon sugar
1 cup milk
3 drops vanilla essence
Nutmeg

1. Have a moderate oven in readiness.
2. Grease a small ovenproof dish with a little butter.
3. Beat the egg with the sugar until thick.
4. Add the milk and vanilla.
5. Pour mixture into the buttered dish.
6. Grate nutmeg on top, and wipe edges of dish.
7. Stand in a baking dish half-full of water; this prevents the custard from curdling while it is cooking.
8. Bake in a slow oven, 150°–160°C, for 15 to 20 minutes or till set (when cooked, a knife-blade inserted in the centre will come out clean)
9. Remove immediately from hot water.

STEAMED CUSTARD

Use baked custard recipe (see p. 67) but cover dish with greased paper and cook in a steamer. Test as above and remove immediately from hot water.

BREAD AND BUTTER CUSTARD

1 tablespoon sultanas
1 thin slice buttered bread
1 egg
1 tablespoon sugar
1¼ cups milk
3 drops vanilla essence
Nutmeg

1. Place prepared sultanas in a greased ovenproof dish.
2. Cut the buttered bread into small squares or finger lengths.
3. Place in dish.
4. Beat egg and sugar together, add milk and essence, and beat well.
5. Pour over bread.
6. Grate nutmeg over top, and wipe edges of dish.
7. Stand in a baking dish half-full of cold water and place in a slow oven, 150°–160°C, and cook till set, from 20 to 30 minutes (when cooked, a knife-blade inserted in the centre will come out clean).
8. Remove immediately from hot water.

STEAMED BREAD AND BUTTER CUSTARD

Use bread and butter custard recipe but cover dish with greased paper and cook in a steamer. Test as above and remove immediately from hot water.

RICE, MACARONI, OR VERMICELLI CUSTARD

1¼ cups water
Pinch salt
1 tablespoon rice, macaroni
    or vermicelli
1 egg
1 tablespoon sugar
1¼ cups milk
3 drops vanilla essence
1 teaspoon butter
Nutmeg

1. Have a moderate oven ready.
2. Put water and salt on to boil.
3. When boiling add cereal.
4. Cook until soft, from 15 to 20 minutes.
5. Beat egg and sugar together, then add milk and vanilla.
6. When cereal is cooked, strain and mix with the custard mixture.
7. Pour into an ovenproof dish, sprinkle with nutmeg, and put small pieces of butter on top.
8. Wipe edges of dish.
9. Stand in a baking dish half-full of cold water, place in a slow oven, 150°–160°C, and bake until set, about 20 to 30 minutes (when cooked, a knife-blade inserted in the centre will come out clean).
10. Remove immediately from hot water.

SAGO CUSTARD

1 tablespoon sago
⅔ cup water
Pinch salt
1 cup milk
1 tablespoon sugar
1 egg
3 drops vanilla essence
Nutmeg
1 teaspoon butter

1. Have a moderate oven in readiness.
2. Wash sago.
3. Put water and pinch of salt on to boil.
4. Place the sago in the boiling water, and stir till it is quite transparent.
5. Add milk and sugar, and stir till well blended with the sago; remove from stove and cool.
6. Beat egg lightly, add with vanilla to the sago when cool.
7. Pour into an ovenproof dish, sprinkle with nutmeg, and place small pieces of butter on top.
8. Wipe edges of dish, and stand it in a baking dish half-full of cold water.
9. Bake in a slow oven, 150°–160°C, till set, about ½ hour (when cooked, a knife-blade inserted in the centre will come out clean).
10. Remove immediately from hot water.

STIRRED CUSTARD (1)

1 cup milk
1 egg
1 tablespoon sugar
4 drops vanilla essence
Nutmeg

1. Warm milk in a double saucepan or in a jug standing in saucepan of water.
2. Beat egg and sugar together until thick; add warm milk.
3. Return to double saucepan or jug.
4. Stir with a wooden spoon till the custard coats the spoon. Do not allow it to overheat or it will curdle.
5. Add vanilla. Cool.
6. Place in a serving dish or in custard glasses, with nutmeg grated on top.

STIRRED CUSTARD (2)

1 teaspoon maize cornflour
1¼ cups milk
1 egg
1 tablespoon sugar
Vanilla essence to taste

1. Blend cornflour with a little of the milk; put remainder of the milk on to boil in a saucepan.
2. When boiling, stir in cornflour, cook for 1 minute; allow to cool off stove.
3. When cool add egg and sugar beaten together; stand saucepan over boiling water and stir till custard coats the spoon (do not let it overheat); add vanilla.

SAGO OR TAPIOCA CREAM

3 tablespoons sago or tapioca
½ cup water
2 cups milk
3 tablespoons sugar
2 eggs
Vanilla essence to taste

1. Soak sago in the cold water for 10 minutes, tapioca overnight.
2. Place in a double saucepan with milk. Cook sago about ¼ hour, or till soft, stirring occasionally; tapioca 1 hour or until clear.
3. Mix sugar and egg yolks, add gradually, and stir a few minutes longer. Remove from stove.
4. Beat whites of eggs stiffly and pour the hot custard onto them gradually, stirring all the time.
5. Add vanilla.
6. When cool, place in serving dish.

QUEEN PUDDING

2 thin slices buttered bread or
     stale sponge cake
Jam
1 egg
2 tablespoons sugar
1 cup milk
Pink sugar (see p. 165)

1. Have a moderate oven in readiness.
2. Spread the buttered bread or sponge cake thinly with jam.
3. Cut in thin strips and place in an ovenproof dish till half filled.
4. Separate the white from the yolk of the egg.
5. Mix the yolk with 1 tablespoon sugar.
6. Warm the milk, but do not overheat.
7. Pour the warm milk onto the yolk and sugar, and mix well together.
8. Pour over bread or cake in dish.
9. Stand the ovenproof dish in a baking dish half-filled with cold water to prevent the custard from boiling while cooking.
10. Cook in a slow oven, $150°-160°C$, till set, about $\frac{1}{2}$ hour.
11. Allow to cool.
12. When cool, spread a thin layer of jam on top.
13. Beat the white of egg to a stiff froth.
14. Add to it 1 tablespoon sugar. Beat till thick.
15. Pile lightly on top of the pudding.
16. Stand in a moderate oven till pale brown.
17. Sprinkle pink sugar on top and serve.

BAKED RICE

2 tablespoons rice
$\frac{2}{3}$ cup water
$1\frac{1}{4}$ cups milk
1 tablespoon sugar
1 teaspoon butter
Nutmeg

1. Wash rice if necessary.
2. Put rice in ovenproof dish, add water, and cook in slow oven until rice absorbs all the water.
3. Add milk, sugar, butter, and grated nutmeg to rice; mix well.
4. Bake in a very slow oven from 1 to $1\frac{1}{2}$ hours.

Note. Rice may be boiled in a saucepan instead of cooked in an ovenproof dish in the oven.

STEAMED OR BOILED PUDDINGS

Steaming

Two methods may be used:

1. Stand covered basin in steamer over a saucepan of gently boiling water.
2. Stand covered basin in saucepan with enough gently boiling water to reach half-way up the side of the basin. It will be necessary with this method to add extra boiling water while cooking—pour gently between the basin and the saucepan.

Boiling

1. Tie a floured pudding cloth firmly over the basin with string, tie opposite corners of cloth together on top. Place in a large saucepan containing enough boiling water to cover the pudding. Boil gently.
2. Tie pudding in a pudding cloth and boil.

APPLE PUDDING

3 apples
2 tablespoons sugar
3 cloves
1 quantity suet crust or short-crust pastry (see pp. 94, 93)
1 strip of lemon rind

1. Peel, quarter, core, and slice the apples.
2. Place on a plate with the sugar and cloves.
3. Put a saucepan of water on to boil.
4. Grease a small basin with butter and sprinkle with sugar.
5. Roll out two-thirds of the pastry into a round shape, and line the basin.
6. Put in the fruit, sugar, cloves and rind, piling high.
7. Wet round the edge of pastry.
8. Roll out the remaining one-third of the pastry, and cover the basin, pressing the edges well together.
9. Pinch a frill around the edge.
10. For steaming cover with greaseproof paper or aluminium foil. For boiling tie a floured cloth firmly over the top of basin.
11. Cook $1\frac{1}{2}$ to 2 hours.
12. Turn onto a hot plate.
13. Serve with suitable sauce or custard.

QUICKLY MADE APPLE PUDDING

6 cooking apples
2 cups water
4 tablespoons sugar
6 cloves
1 piece lemon rind
Double quantity suet crust or
    shortcrust pastry (see
    pp. 94, 93,)

1. Peel, core, and quarter apples.
2. Boil water, sugar, cloves and lemon rind, add apples and cook gently with lid on.
3. Roll out the pastry to size of the saucepan lid. Make a hole in the centre.
4. Place in saucepan on top of boiling apples.
5. Cook gently with the lid on 20 to 30 minutes.
6. Lift out pastry, cut into triangles and serve with apples on a hot plate.

CHRISTMAS PUDDING

500 g currants
500 g sultanas
250 g raisins
250 g citron peel
125 g almonds
500 g butter
500 g brown sugar
9 eggs
$\frac{2}{3}$ cup brandy
250 g breadcrumbs
250 g plain flour
Pinch salt
1 teaspoon bicarbonate of soda
$\frac{1}{2}$ nutmeg or $\frac{1}{2}$ teaspoon grated nutmeg
2 teaspoons mixed spice

1. Clean and prepare all the fruit, cut the citron peel finely, blanch and chop the almonds.
2. Have a large boiler of water in readiness.
3. Cream the butter and sugar, add well-beaten eggs and brandy.
4. Stir all the fruit in well.
5. Add breadcrumbs, sifted flour, salt, soda, grated nutmeg, and spice.
6. Mix all well together.
7. Tie up in a very strong pudding cloth, allowing room for it to swell.
8. Place in boiling water and cook 6 hours. Cook a further 3 hours on the day it is to be eaten.
9. Serve with brandy or wine sauce, or stirred custard.

Note. This mixture may be steamed in one large or two medium basins. Allow 4 cm at the top of the basin for swelling. Steam large pudding 6 hours first day and 3 hours on day to be eaten; half-size puddings, 4 hours first day, $1\frac{1}{2}$ hours on day of eating.

COLLEGE PUDDING

1 tablespoon jam
1 cup self-raising flour
$\frac{1}{4}$ cup sugar
1 egg
Pinch salt
$\frac{1}{4}$ cup butter, clarified fat, or
    margarine
3 tablespoons milk
4 drops vanilla essence

1. Place a saucepan of water on to boil, over which the pudding is to steam.
2. Grease a mould with butter, and put the jam in the bottom of it.
3. Cut a piece of greaseproof paper or foil the same shape as the top of the mould, but 3 cm larger than it all round.
4. Sift the flour and salt.
5. Beat the butter and sugar to a cream.
6. Beat the egg and add it gradually to the butter and sugar, beating well.
7. Stir in the milk and the vanilla.
8. Stir in the flour lightly.
9. Pour the mixture into the mould, and cover with the greased paper or foil.
10. Place in the steamer and steam $1\frac{1}{2}$ hours.
11. Turn out of the mould onto a hot dish, and serve with jam or white sauce.

GOLDEN TOP PUDDING

Use recipe for College Pudding but omit jam and replace with 2 tablespoons of honey or golden syrup.

CHOCOLATE PUDDING

Use recipe for College Pudding but omit jam. Add 1 tablespoon of cocoa to the flour and 1 extra tablespoon of milk.

ORANGE OR LEMON PUDDING

Use recipe for College Pudding but omit jam. Add 1 teaspoon of grated orange or lemon rind and 1 teaspoon of juice to the mixture.

EGGLESS PUDDING

An eggless, sugarless pudding

1 tablespoon margarine
$\frac{1}{4}$ teaspoon bicarbonate of soda
2 tablespoons golden syrup
$\frac{1}{2}$ cup milk
1 cup self-raising flour
$\frac{1}{4}$ teaspoon spice

1. Melt margarine in a basin standing in hot water.
2. Dissolve the bicarbonate of soda and golden syrup in milk and add to margarine.
3. Sift flour and spice.
4. Stir into above mixture till a smooth consistency.
5. Place into greased moulds.
6. Cover with greased paper.
7. Steam 1 hour.

This mixture is sufficient for 4. Cocoa, sultanas, dates, etc. may be added for variety.

SAGO FRUIT PUDDING

4 tablespoons sago
1 cup milk
$\frac{1}{4}$ cup butter
$\frac{1}{2}$ cup sugar
1 teaspoon bicarbonate of soda
1 cup fresh breadcrumbs
$\frac{1}{4}$ cup plain flour
$\frac{1}{4}$ teaspoon salt
$\frac{1}{2}$ cup sultanas
$\frac{1}{2}$ cup raisins
$\frac{1}{2}$ cup chopped dates

1. Soak sago in milk overnight.
2. Place saucepan of water on to boil over which the pudding is to steam.
3. Grease mould with butter and cut a piece of greaseproof paper or foil the same shape as the top of the mould, but 3 cm larger all round.
4. Beat butter and sugar.
5. Add sago and milk with soda.
6. Add breadcrumbs, sifted flour, salt, and fruit and mix all lightly.
7. Place in prepared mould, cover with greaseproof paper or foil, and steam for $2\frac{1}{2}$ hours to 3 hours.
8. Serve with suitable sauce or custard.

STEAMED DATE, SULTANA, OR CURRANT PUDDING

1 cup dates, sultanas, or currants
$\frac{1}{4}$ cup butter, clarified fat, or margarine
$\frac{1}{4}$ cup sugar
1 egg (60 g)
3 tablespoons milk
1 cup self-raising flour
Pinch salt

1. Place a saucepan of water on to boil, over which the pudding is to steam.
2. Grease a mould with butter.
3. Cut a piece of greaseproof paper or foil the same shape as the top of the mould, but 3 cm larger all round.
4. Stone the dates and cut them into four — wash and dry sultanas or currants.
5. Beat the butter and sugar to a cream.
6. Beat the egg well and add it to the butter and sugar gradually, beating until thick.
7. Add the milk.
8. Add the dates or dried fruit.
9. Sift the flour and salt, and add to the other ingredients.
10. Stir in very lightly.
11. Turn into the mould, cover with the paper or foil.
12. Steam $1\frac{1}{2}$ hours.
13. Turn onto a hot plate and serve with white sauce or custard.

STEAMED JAM ROLL

$1\frac{1}{2}$ cups self-raising flour
Pinch salt
$\frac{1}{4}$ cup butter, clarified fat, or margarine
3 tablespoons water or milk
Jam

1. Place a saucepan of water on to boil, over which the pudding is to steam.
2. Grease a pudding basin, and have a piece of greaseproof paper or foil cut a little larger than the top of the basin.
3. Sift the flour and salt.
4. Rub in the butter with the tips of the fingers.
5. Mix into a rather stiff dough with the water or milk.
6. Lift onto a floured board and press into a round shape.
7. Roll out 5 mm thickness and spread with jam to within 3 cm of the edge all round.
8. Roll up lightly.

(continued)

Egg and Bacon Pie (p. 57) with tossed salad (p. 44).

9. Place into the prepared basin.
10. Cover with the paper or foil.
11. Steam 1½ hours.
12. Turn out onto a hot plate with jam sauce (see p.142).

URNEY PUDDING

1 cup plain flour
Pinch salt
¼ cup butter, margarine or dripping
¼ cup sugar
1 egg
3 tablespoons milk
½ teaspoon bicarbonate of soda
1 tablespoon jam

1. Place a saucepan of water on to boil, over which the pudding is to steam.
2. Grease a pudding mould with butter.
3. Cut a piece of greaseproof paper or foil the same shape as the top of the mould but 3 cm larger all round.
4. Sift the flour and salt.
5. Beat the butter and sugar to a cream in a basin.
6. Beat the egg, add to butter and sugar, and beat well.
7. Stir in the milk, soda, and jam.
8. Stir in the sifted flour.
9. Turn into the mould and cover with the paper or foil.
10. Steam 1½ hours.
11. Turn out of the mould onto a hot plate and serve with sauce or stirred custard (see p. 70).

GINGER PUDDING

Use recipe for Urney Pudding but substitute golden syrup for jam and add 3 teaspoons of ground ginger with the flour.

Stewed Rhubard, Stewed Pears.

SUMMER PUDDINGS

APPLE AND RICE MERINGUE

Apple

4 apples
4 tablespoons sugar
$\frac{2}{3}$ cup water
4 cloves

1. Peel, core, and quarter apples.
2. Boil sugar and water; add cloves and apples.
3. Cook gently with lid on till tender, then place in a fireproof dish.

Rice

$\frac{1}{4}$ cup rice
3 cups boiling water
Pinch salt
1 egg yolk (60 g)
2 tablespoons sugar
$\frac{2}{3}$ cup milk

1. Place rice into a saucepan containing the boiling water and salt. Boil 15 minutes or until soft. Strain.
2. Return to saucepan, and add egg yolk, sugar, and milk. Stir, and cook 3 minutes.
3. Pour this mixture over the cooked apple or make it into a border.

Meringue

1 egg white
Pinch salt
2 tablespoons sugar
1 teaspoon pink sugar (see p. 165)

1. Beat egg white stiffly, adding salt.
2. Stir in the sugar. Beat well.
3. Heap this up roughly on top of the pudding.
4. Place in a slow oven or under griller until lightly browned.
5. Sprinkle the pink sugar over the top.

APPLE SNOW

4 cooking apples
4 tablespoons sugar
2 cloves
Small piece lemon rind
Cochineal
3 tablespoons water
1 or 2 egg whites

1. Peel, core, and slice apples thinly.
2. Place them in a saucepan with the sugar, cloves, lemon rind, cochineal, and water.
3. Stew gently till the apples are quite tender. Drain well.
4. Beat to a pulp.
5. Beat up the egg whites to a stiff froth.
6. Add gradually to apple pulp, beating well till white and spongy.
7. Chill.
8. Serve with stirred custard (see p. 70), which may be made from the egg yolks.

Note. Pulped apricots, peaches, prunes, or berries may be used instead of apple.

APPLE SPONGE

6 cooking apples
1 cup water
6 tablespoons sugar
2 cloves
Cake mixture
2 tablespoons butter
$\frac{1}{4}$ cup sugar
1 egg
$\frac{2}{3}$ cup milk
3 drops vanilla essence
1 cup self-raising flour
Pinch salt
Icing sugar

1. Have a moderate oven in readiness.
2. Peel, quarter, and core the apples.
3. Place in a saucepan with the water, 6 tablespoons sugar, and cloves.
4. Cook till the apples are tender.
5. Pour into an ovenproof dish.
6. Beat the butter and $\frac{1}{4}$ cup sugar to a cream.
7. Add beaten egg gradually, and beat until the mixture thickens.
8. Add milk and vanilla.
9. Sift flour and salt, stir in lightly and quickly.
10. Pour this mixture over the hot stewed apples.
11. Bake in a moderate oven, 180°C, about $\frac{1}{2}$ hour.
12. Sprinkle icing sugar on the top.
13. Serve with custard, cream, or ice-cream.

BAKED APPLE AMBER PUDDING

6 apples
$\frac{1}{3}$ cup sugar
A few cloves
2 tablespoons water
Rind of half lemon
1 tablespoon lemon juice
2 eggs
$\frac{1}{4}$ cup butter
1 quantity shortcrust pastry
    (see p. 93)
2 tablespoons   sugar   for
    meringue

1. Peel, core, and slice the apples, place in a saucepan with sugar, cloves, water, grated lemon rind and lemon juice, and cook gently until tender.
2. When cooked beat until smooth.
3. Separate whites from yolks of eggs; stir yolks and butter in the apple mixture.
4. Roll pastry thinly, and cut into strips. Line edges only of pie-dish, ornament with a spoon or leaves of pastry partly overlapping. Glaze well to hold them together.
5. Pour in the prepared mixture, and bake in a moderate oven, 180°–200°C, until set and the pastry turns a pale fawn colour.
6. Whisk the whites of the eggs until quite stiff, adding sugar gradually.
7. Place roughly on top of the pudding, and return to oven until set and lightly browned.

BAKED APRICOT PUDDING

4 tablespoons   fine   white
    breadcrumbs
4 tablespoons sugar
2 cups milk
1 can (250g) apricots or
    stewed apricots
3 eggs (60 g)

1. Mix breadcrumbs and sugar.
2. Boil milk and pour onto breadcrumbs. Allow to stand for $\frac{1}{2}$ hour.
3. Grease an ovenproof dish.
4. Place the apricots and a little of the syrup ($\frac{1}{2}$ cup) in the pie-dish.
5. Beat the 3 egg yolks and 1 egg white together.
6. Add to breadcrumbs and milk, mix thoroughly, and pour onto the apricots.
7. Bake in a moderate oven, 160°–180°C, until mixture sets.
8. Beat remaining egg whites stiffly, add sugar, and beat again until stiff and frothy, then pile roughly on top of pudding.
9. Return to oven for a few minutes to set white of egg.
10. Serve hot or cold.

Note. Sliced peaches or pineapple cubes may be substituted for the apricots.

BANANA CUSTARD

2 ripe bananas
Jam or 2 tablespoons lemon
    juice
1 quantity stirred custard (see
    p. 70).
Nutmeg

1. Peel and slice bananas.
2. Place in a dish.
3. Spread jam or fruit juice on bananas.
4. Pour custard over.
5. Grate nutmeg on top.

CHOCOLATE SAUCE PUDDING

$\frac{1}{4}$ cup butter or margarine
$\frac{1}{2}$ cup sugar
1 egg (60 g)
1 cup self-raising flour
1 tablespoon cocoa
$\frac{1}{2}$ cup milk
Extra $\frac{1}{2}$ cup sugar
Extra $1\frac{1}{2}$ tablespoons cocoa
$1\frac{1}{2}$ cups hot water

1. Cream butter and sugar.
2. Add egg and beat well.
3. Fold in sifted flour and cocoa alternately with milk.
4. Place mixture into a greased ovenproof dish.
5. Mix extra sugar and cocoa together and sprinkle over mixture.
6. Pour hot water over carefully.
7. Bake in a moderate oven, $180°–190°C$, 35 to 40 minutes.

FRUIT FLUMMERY

2 tablespoons gelatine
1 cup hot water
2 tablespoons flour
1 cup sugar
$\frac{1}{2}$ cup orange juice
1 tablespoon lemon juice
$\frac{2}{3}$ cup passionfruit pulp
1 or 2 egg whites (optional)

1. Dissolve gelatine in $\frac{1}{4}$ cup hot water.
2. Blend flour with a little cold water, and carefully add to remaining hot water. Add sugar and stir over heat for 3 to 5 minutes.
3. When cooled slightly add dissolved gelatine.
4. Add orange and lemon juice.
5. Turn into a basin and when thickening slightly beat until very thick and foamy.
6. Add passionfruit pulp and stiffly beaten egg whites. Pour into a serving dish.

Note. Use egg yolks for stirred custard (see p. 70).

FRUIT SALAD

1 small pineapple
6 passionfruit
2 pears
3 peaches
3 bananas
A few strawberries
$\frac{1}{4}$ cup sugar
Cream or custard
Icing sugar

1. Peel the pineapple and grate or cut up finely into a basin.
2. Cut passionfruit in halves and scoop out contents.
3. Peel peaches and pears thinly, using a silver or stainless steel knife and fork. Cut them finely and add to pineapple and passionfruit.
4. Peel bananas, cut in rings, and add with strawberries to other fruit.
5. Sprinkle sugar over fruit, and mix all well together.
6. Place in a salad bowl or glass dish, and let stand 1 hour to allow a syrup to form and the flavours to blend together.
7. Serve with cream or custard, and icing sugar.

Note. Any ripe fruit may be used in a salad if carefully prepared.

LEMON PUDDING

3 tablespoons cornflour
1 egg (60 g)
$1\frac{1}{4}$ cups water
2 tablespoons sugar
1 teaspoon grated lemon rind
1 tablespoon butter
4 tablespoons lemon juice
Extra 1 tablespoon sugar for egg white

1. Blend cornflour with a little of the water.
2. Separate yolk from white of egg.
3. Place remainder of water, sugar, and lemon rind on to boil.
4. When boiling stir in blended cornflour, cook 3 minutes, then stir in the butter, egg yolk and lemon juice.
5. Pour the mixture into an ovenproof dish and allow to cool.
6. Beat egg white stiffly, add 1 tablespoon sugar, beat well.
7. Heap roughly on top of lemon mixture.
8. Bake in a slow oven until meringue is set and lightly browned.
9. Serve cold with custard.

Note. 1 cup of canned crushed pineapple may be substituted for lemon.

LEMON SAUCE PUDDING

2 eggs (60 g)
2 tablespoons butter
$\frac{3}{4}$ cup sugar
2 tablespoons   self-raising
    flour
Pinch salt
1 teaspoon grated lemon rind
$\frac{1}{3}$ cup lemon juice
1 cup milk

1. Separate whites from yolks of eggs.
2. Cream butter and sugar.
3. Add sifted flour and salt.
4. Add grated lemon rind, lemon juice, egg yolks, and milk.
5. Beat egg whites until stiff, and fold into mixture.
6. Pour into greased ovenproof dish, and stand in a dish of cold water.
7. Bake in a moderate oven, 180°–200°C, for 40 minutes.

LEMON SAGO

$\frac{1}{3}$ cup sago
2 cups water
Pinch salt
1 teaspoon grated lemon rind
2 tablespoons lemon juice
1 tablespoon golden syrup
2 tablespoons brown sugar

1. Wash sago; soak for 1 hour in the water.
2. Drain off water into saucepan, and put on to boil with pinch of salt.
3. When boiling, add the sago and stir till quite transparent.
4. Add lemon rind and lemon juice, also syrup and sugar.
5. Pour into wetted moulds and chill.
6. Turn out when set.
7. Serve with stirred custard (see p. 70).

PASSIONFRUIT SHAPE

5 tablespoons cornflour
1 egg (55 g or 60 g)
$2\frac{1}{2}$ cups milk
$\frac{1}{2}$ cup sugar
1 tablespoon butter
4 passionfruit

1. Blend cornflour with a little of the milk.
2. Separate yolk from white of egg.
3. Place remainder of milk and sugar on to boil.
4. Stir in blended cornflour; cook 3 minutes.
5. Add butter and egg yolk, stir, and cook gently 1 minute.
6. Fold in stiffly beaten egg white and then the passionfruit pulp.
7. Set in a wet mould and chill.
8. Serve with custard, cream, or ice-cream.

CREAMED RICE SHAPE

$\frac{1}{2}$ cup rice
$\frac{1}{2}$ cup water
Pinch salt
2 cups milk
1 cinnamon stick (optional)
A strip of lemon rind
4 tablespoons sugar
A little lemon essence

1. Wash rice if necessary.
2. Put into a saucepan with the water and salt.
3. Cook until water is absorbed.
4. Add milk, cinnamon, and lemon rind.
5. Cook gently until grain is soft and nearly dry.
6. Remove cinnamon and rind.
7. Add sugar and essence.
8. Pour into a wet mould.
9. Chill and serve.

Note. 1 tablespoon gelatine soaked in 3 tablespoons of hot water may be added to the rice just before it is poured into the mould to make the shape set firmly.

SWEET POACHED EGGS

6 halves of preserved or stewed apricots
1 quantity blancmange (see p. 67)

1. Place each half apricot in a cup or small mould, keeping skin side downwards.
2. Pour over sufficient blancmange to well cover the apricot.
3. Set aside till cold, turn out onto a serving dish.

FRUITS—STEWED AND CASSEROLED

STEWED FRUIT

Fruit should retain its shape while cooking.

Choose saucepan large enough for quantity of fruit. If packed too high fruit will cook unevenly and break.

The quantity of sugar will vary according to personal taste.

Simmer gently in a small quantity of liquid with the lid fitted tightly on the saucepan.

After removing the fruit, syrup may be coloured with a few drops of vegetable colouring. It may be thickened with a little blended arrowroot or soaked sago. It may be boiled quickly without the lid for a few minutes to reduce the quantity.

STEWED APPLES OR PEARS

4 cooking apples or pears
4 tablespoons sugar
2 cloves or a strip of lemon peel.

1. Peel the fruit very thinly, cut in quarters, and remove the cores.
2. Put 1–2 cm of water in a saucepan, add sugar and cloves, and bring to boil.
3. When boiling, add the fruit.
4. Cook gently with the lid on till tender.
5. Allow to cool, remove the cloves or peel.

CASSEROLED APPLES OR PEARS

4 apples or pears
4 tablespoons sugar
3 passionfruit

1. Heat oven.
2. Grease a casserole dish with butter.
3. Peel, quarter, and core the fruit.
4. Place peeled side up in the casserole, and add sugar and 1 cm of water.
5. Cover with the lid and bake very slowly, 150°–160°C, until soft (about 1 hour).
6. Serve with passionfruit pulp on top of the fruit.

STEWED DRIED APRICOTS

250 g dried apricots
2 cups water
2 tablespoons sugar

1. Wash apricots.
2. Soak in cold water 12 hours or until soft.
3. Strain liquid off into a saucepan.
4. Add the sugar and bring to the boil.
5. Add apricots.
6. Cook very slowly with lid on for 10 minutes, or till tender.

STEWED PEACHES, APRICOTS, PLUMS, OR NECTARINES

6 pieces of fruit
4 tablespoons sugar

1. Wash fruit and peel if necessary.
2. Put 1–2 cm of water in a saucepan, add sugar and bring to boil.
3. When boiling, add the fruit.
4. Cook gently with the lid on till quite tender, about 10 to 15 minutes.

STEWED PRUNES

250 g prunes
1½ cups water
2 tablespoons sugar
Strip of lemon rind

1. Soak prunes in water.
2. Strain liquid off into a saucepan.
3. Add the sugar and lemon rind, and bring to boil.
4. Add prunes.
5. Cook very slowly with lid on till tender, about 10 to 15 minutes.
6. Remove lemon rind and serve.

Note. If prunes are soft and do not require soaking, use ½ cup of water.

STEWED QUINCES

2 large quinces
½ cup sugar

1. Wash and dry quinces, peel thinly, quarter and core them.
2. Drop into a basin of cold water to keep their colour.
3. Put 5–7 cm of water in a saucepan, add sugar, and bring to boil.
4. Add the quinces and cook gently until they are quite soft and beginning to turn pink, about 1 to 2 hours.
5. Allow to cool.

Note. Using a pressure cooker, at low pressure, will reduce cooking time to approximately 30 minutes.

STEWED RHUBARB

1 bunch rhubarb
¼ cup water
4 tablespoons sugar
1 pinch ground ginger or 1 teaspoon lemon juice.

1. Cut the leaves off the rhubarb, and trim ends of stalks.
2. Wash well.
3. Cut into pieces about 3 cm long.
4. Put water, sugar, and ginger or lemon juice on to boil.
5. When boiling, add rhubarb.
6. Cook gently with the lid on till tender; about 10 to 15 minutes.
7. Allow to cool.

CASSEROLED RHUBARB

1 tablespoon sago
1 bunch rhubarb
¾ cup sugar
A little grated lemon rind

1. Soak the sago in 1 cm of water in a casserole for half an hour.
2. Wash and dry the rhubarb and cut it into pieces 3 cm long.
3. Place in the casserole with the sugar and lemon rind.
4. Cover with lid and bake very slowly for half an hour.
5. Cool and serve.

BATTERS

BATTER FOR FISH, MEAT, OR SAVOURY DISHES

1 cup plain flour
Pinch salt
1 egg yolk
$\frac{2}{3}$ cup milk

1. Sift flour and salt.
2. Make a well in the centre.
3. Pour in egg yolk.
4. Stir lightly.
5. Add milk gradually.
6. Beat well to make batter smooth and light.
7. Allow to stand about $\frac{1}{2}$ hour before using.

ECONOMICAL BATTER

1 cup self-raising flour
Pinch salt
$\frac{2}{3}$ cup milk

1. Sift flour and salt.
2. Make a well in middle of flour.
3. Add milk gradually and mix with wooden spoon until smooth.

FRITTER BATTER

1 cup self-raising flour
Pinch salt
1 tablespoon melted butter or oil
$\frac{2}{3}$ cup tepid water (2 parts cold, 1 part boiling)
1 egg white

1. Sift flour and salt into a basin.
2. Make a well in the middle.
3. Pour in oil or butter.
4. Stir flour in gradually with back of a wooden spoon.
5. Add water, a little at a time.
6. Beat into a smooth batter.
7. Beat egg white stiffly.
8. Stir it in very lightly last of all, just before using.

Note. This may be used for all kinds of fruit fritters. Add 1 tablespoon castor sugar for sweet batter.

BANANA FRITTERS

4 bananas
1 quantity fritter batter
Frying fat or oil
Icing sugar

1. Peel bananas and cut into 4 pieces.
2. Add bananas to fritter batter, mix in very lightly.
3. Wet fry a golden brown colour.
4. Drain on absorbent paper.
5. Serve on a hot dish or plate. Sprinkle with icing sugar.

BATTER FOR PANCAKES, ETC.

1 cup plain flour
Pinch salt
1 egg
$1\frac{1}{4}$ cups milk

1. Sift flour and salt.
2. Break egg and remove the speck.
3. Make a well in the middle of the flour.
4. Add egg (whole).
5. Stir in flour gradually from the sides.
6. Add milk, a little at a time.
7. When half the milk is used, all the flour must be moistened.
8. Beat well to remove all lumps and make it light.
9. When quite smooth, add the remainder of the milk gradually.
10. Stand it aside for 1 hour.

Note. This batter may also be used for Yorkshire pudding and sausages in batter.

PANCAKES

Pancake batter
$1\frac{1}{2}$ tablespoons butter
1 lemon
1 tablespoon sugar

1. Measure carefully 2 tablespoons of batter into a mug or cup.
2. Prepare omelet pan as follows: Put a small piece of butter or fat in the pan, burn it and wipe quite dry with a small piece of kitchen paper, put another small piece of butter in pan, melt it.
3. Pour measured amount of batter into the pan, and allow it to spread evenly over by moving the pan about.

(continued)

4. Cook quickly till set and slightly brown.
5. Loosen edges with a knife.
6. Toss or turn pancake with a knife, and cook on other side till brown.
7. Drain on absorbent paper.
8. Melt a little more butter in pan, measure batter, and pour in as before.
9. While this is setting, sprinkle lemon juice and sugar on the one on the paper, fold it up, and put on a plate. Keep hot over a saucepan of boiling water, to prevent drying.
10. Serve as soon as possible on a hot dish, with thin slices of lemon, and sugar sprinkled over.

Note. Jam or savoury spreads may be used instead of lemon and sugar.

YORKSHIRE PUDDING

Pancake batter (see pp. 89)
2 tablespoons clarified fat

1. Heat clarified fat in a cake pan or baking dish.
2. Pour batter in.
3. Bake in a moderate oven, 180°–190°C, for 20 to 30 minutes according to thickness.
4. Drain the fat out of the pan; cut pudding into triangle or squares.
5. Serve as an accompaniment to roast beef.

Note. If meat is placed on a trivet, the mixture can be cooked in the baking dish under the meat.

PASTRY

BISCUIT OR CHAMPAGNE PASTRY

$1\frac{1}{4}$ cups self-raising flour
1 tablespoon cornflour
Pinch salt
$\frac{1}{3}$ cup butter
1 egg (60 g)
$\frac{1}{4}$ cup sugar

1. Sift self-raising flour, cornflour, and salt.
2. Rub in the butter.
3. Mix into a dry dough with beaten egg and sugar.
4. Turn onto a floured board, and roll out lightly.
5. Use as required for sweet dishes.
6. Bake in a moderate oven, 180°–200°C, for about 25 minutes.

CHOUX PASTRY

$\frac{1}{4}$ cup butter
$1\frac{1}{4}$ cups water
1 cup plain flour
3 large eggs (60 g)

1. Grease scone tray.
2. Boil butter and water in a saucepan.
3. Remove from stove, stir in sifted flour all at once and beat till smooth.
4. Beat well over heat and cook until it leaves the sides of the saucepan (do not undercook).
5. Allow to cool slightly (no more than 5 minutes).
6. Whisk eggs well.
7. Beat into mixture.
8. Use as required.
9. Bake in a hot oven, 220°–250°C, for $\frac{1}{2}$ hour in gradually decreasing heat.
10. Do not open oven door for at least 10 minutes.

Note: Choux pastry may be used for savoury and sweet puffs and eclairs.

FLAKY PASTRY

1 cup plain flour
½ teaspoon baking powder
¼ teaspoon salt
⅛ teaspoon sugar (for sweet pastry)
¼ cup clarified fat, lard, or margarine
3 tablespoons water

1. Sift the flour, baking powder, salt, and sugar (if used).
2. Soften the fat, and divide into four.
3. Rub one fourth into the flour.
4. Add the water nearly all at once, adding a little more water if necessary to make into a dough the same consistency as the fat.
5. Turn onto a slightly floured board.
6. Knead well to an even consistency.
7. Roll out, away from you, into a thin oblong shape.
8. Spread another fourth of the fat on, leaving a margin about 2 cm wide all round the edge of the dough.
9. Sprinkle a little flour over,
10. Fold in 3 even folds, one on top of the other, and draw the edges well together.
11. Turn the dough half round so that an open end faces you.
12. Roll out straight from you.
13. Add another fourth of fat, repeat folding and rolling as before.
14. Spread on remaining fourth of fat, fold, and roll out again.
15. Fold in three without fat, roll to size and shape required.

PUFF PASTRY

250 g (1 cup) butter
2 cups plain flour
⅛ teaspoon salt
1 egg
Squeeze of lemon juice
⅔ cup cold water

1. Squeeze the butter in a dry cloth to remove all the moisture.
2. Make into an oblong pat about 2.5 cm thick and put in refrigerator.
3. Sift the flour and salt.
4. Separate yolk from white of egg. Beat the yolk, water, and lemon juice together, and add to flour.
5. Make into a soft but not sticky dough, and turn onto a floured board.

(continued)

Strawberry Pancakes (pancake batter p. 89).

6. Knead well and roll out square about 1 cm thick.
7. Put the pat of butter on one side of the pastry.
8. Wet round the edge of the pastry, fold over the butter, and pinch a frill round.
9. Turn the pastry so that the fold is at the right hand side, and roll the pastry out into a thin sheet, rolling from you only.
10. Fold in three, turn so that an open end faces you, and roll out from you only.
11. Fold and put aside in refrigerator for 10 minutes.
12. Roll and fold twice again and stand in refrigerator for 10 minutes.
13. Do this until the pastry has been folded seven times.
14. Roll to the shape and size required.
15. Glaze with egg white.
16. Bake in a very hot oven, 230°–260°C, for about 20 minutes, and do not open the oven door until the pastry has been in 10 minutes.
17. When cooked put on a cooler to cool.

SHORTCRUST PASTRY

1 cup plain flour
$\frac{1}{2}$ teaspoon baking powder
$\frac{1}{4}$ teaspoon salt
1 teaspoon sugar (if used for fruit pies)
$\frac{1}{4}$ cup clarified fat, lard, or margarine
2 tablespoons water

1. Sift the flour, baking powder, salt, and sugar (if used).
2. Rub in the fat with the tips of the fingers till the mixture looks like breadcrumbs, lifting it well out of the basin during the process to admit the air.
3. Add the water gradually, making into a very dry dough. Do not add all the water unless necessary.
4. Turn onto a slightly floured board.
5. Roll to shape and size required.

Christmas Cake (p. 104).

SUET CRUST

$\frac{1}{4}$ cup suet
1 cup self-raising flour
$\frac{1}{8}$ teaspoon salt
2 tablespoons water or milk

1. Skin, flake, and grate or chop suet very finely.
2. Sift flour, and salt.
3. Add suet; rub well into flour with tips of fingers.
4. Add water gradually, making a very dry dough. Do not add all water unless necessary.
5. Put pastry on a floured board.
6. Knead slightly till smooth.
7. Roll out to size and shape required.

Note. Suet crust is best steamed or boiled.

SWEET PASTRY

BAKED APPLE DUMPLINGS

4 apples
2 teaspoons butter
2 tablespoons sugar
4 cloves
1 teaspoon grated lemon rind
1 quantity shortcrust pastry
    (see p. 93)
Water and sugar for glazing
Icing sugar

1. Have a hot oven in readiness.
2. Peel each apple, thinly, removing core without breaking fruit.
3. Fill up the hole with a little butter, sugar, and a clove and lemon rind.
4. Cut pastry into 4 equal parts.
5. Smooth and roll each into a round shape large enough to come halfway up the apple.
6. Place an apple on each piece, and work the pastry around it with floured palms, until apple is covered.
7. Glaze with water and sugar and place on a slide.
8. Place in hot oven, 220°–230°C, and cook for 30 minutes, gradually decreasing the heat.
9. Test with skewer; if cooked, apple is soft.
10. Lift onto suitable dish, sprinkle with icing sugar, and serve hot or cold with cream or custard.

APPLE PIE

4 cooking apples
4 tablespoons sugar
2 cloves
$\frac{1}{2}$ teaspoon grated lemon rind
1 quantity flaky pastry or shortcrust pastry (see pp. 92, 93)
White of egg or water and sugar for glazing
Icing sugar

1. Peel, quarter, and core the apples.
2. Slice into a pie-dish, adding sugar, cloves, and grated rind, in layers. (If using shortcrust pastry, cook fruit before putting into pie-dish.)
3. Heap up well towards the centre.
4. Roll out pastry in the shape of the pie-dish, 2.5 cm larger.
5. Cut a strip off all round.

(continued)

6. Wet the edge of the dish and put the strip on, the cut edge outward.
7. Brush with water, and put the remainder of the pastry on.
8. Trim the edges, using a sharp knife, cutting from you.
9. Make an incision in the top of pastry to allow steam to escape.
10. Glaze by brushing with white of egg or with water and sugar.
11. Bake in a hot oven, 220°–260°C, until brown, about 20 minutes. If raw apples have been used, reduce temperature after 20 minutes and cook until they are soft.
12. Sprinkle with icing sugar and serve.

Note. Rhubarb, blackberries, peaches or apricots can be substituted for apples.

BUTTERSCOTCH PIE

1 quantity biscuit or champagne pastry (see p. 91)
2 tablespoons butter
$\frac{3}{4}$ cup brown sugar
3 tablespoons maize cornflour
$\frac{3}{4}$ cup milk
2 eggs
$\frac{1}{4}$ teaspoon vanilla
4 tablespoons white sugar

1. Line tart-plate with prepared pastry.
2. Melt butter and brown sugar in saucepan.
3. Blend cornflour with a little of the milk.
4. Heat remainder of milk but do not boil.
5. Add hot milk slowly to butter and sugar, and stir over low heat till combined.
6. Separate yolks from whites of eggs.
7. Combine yolks with blended cornflour and milk.
8. Add to saucepan stirring all the time. Stir in vanilla.
9. Pour into pastry-lined tart-plate.
10. Bake at 200°–220°C until set—about 20 minutes.
11. Beat egg whites till stiff, then gradually add sugar and beat till thick.
12. Pile roughly on top of pie and brown lightly in the oven.

CHEESECAKE

1 quantity shortcrust pastry
    (see p. 93)
2 eggs
125 g (1 cup) cream cheese
$\frac{1}{4}$ cup sugar
1 tablespoon plain flour
$\frac{1}{2}$ teaspoon vanilla essence

1. Line an 18 cm tart-plate with pastry and bake for 15 to 20 minutes at 190°–220°C.
2. Separate whites from yolks of eggs.
3. To egg yolks add cream cheese, sugar, flour and vanilla essence. Mix well.
4. Beat whites of eggs till stiff. Fold into mixture.
5. Put into pastry.
6. Bake in a moderate oven, 180°–200°C, until set—about 15 to 20 minutes.

CUSTARD TART

2 eggs
2 tablespoons sugar
$1\frac{1}{4}$ cups milk
3 drops vanilla essence
1 quantity shortcrust pastry
    (see p. 93)
1 tablespoon jam
Nutmeg

1. Break eggs. Set aside a little of the white from one egg.
2. Beat eggs and sugar; then add the milk and vanilla.
3. Roll out pastry 2 cm larger than tart-plate.
4. Place plate on pastry, and cut round with a sharp knife.
5. Wet edge of plate, and place pastry strips on with cut side out. Glaze, cover with large piece of pastry, and trim edge.
6. Ornament round the edge, and brush the edge and bottom with the remaining egg white.
7. Spread with jam.
8. Fill centre with the custard—pour in slowly.
9. Grate nutmeg on top.
10. Bake in a moderate oven, 180°–200°C, till set—about 20 to 30 minutes.

BAKED JAM ROLL

1 quantity shortcrust pastry
    (see p. 93)
1 cup water
$\frac{1}{4}$ cup sugar
1 tablespoon butter
Jam

1. Grease a deep fireproof dish.
2. Knead and roll out shortcrust pastry 5 cm in thickness.
3. Wet edge of pastry with water or milk.
4. Spread pastry with jam.

(continued)

5. Roll up, press edges together and put into dish.
6. Boil water, sugar, and butter for the sauce.
7. Pour slowly over roll.
8. Bake at 200°–220° C for about $\frac{1}{2}$ hour.

Note. Well-drained fruit may be used instead of jam.

QUICKLY MADE LEMON CHEESE TART

1 quantity shortcrust pastry (see p. 93)
1 tablespoon butter
$\frac{3}{4}$ cup sugar
1 egg
Juice and rind of 1 large lemon

1. Line an 18 × 3 cm tart-plate with pastry.
2. Cream butter and sugar.
3. Add egg, lemon rind, and juice; beat well.
4. Pour into uncooked pastry shell.
5. Bake in a moderate oven, 180°–200° C, for 20 to 30 minutes.

CRUMB CRUST LEMON CREAM PIE

1 cup plain sweet biscuits
$\frac{1}{2}$ cup butter
$\frac{1}{2}$ tin condensed milk
$\frac{1}{2}$ cup lemon juice
$\frac{2}{3}$ cup cream
Cinnamon or nutmeg

1. Crush biscuits.
2. Melt butter, add to biscuits, and press firmly into a tart plate.
3. Bake for 5 minutes at 150°–160° C. Cool.
4. Place condensed milk in a bowl.
5. Add lemon juice gradually and allow to stand a few minutes.
6. Beat the cream, fold through the mixture.
7. Put into biscuit case and refrigerate. Sprinkle lightly with cinnamon or nutmeg before serving.

LEMON MERINGUE TART

2 tablespoons plain flour
2 tablespoons cornflour
$\frac{1}{2}$ cup white sugar
$\frac{1}{2}$ cup lemon juice
1 cup boiling water
2 egg yolks
1 tablespoon butter
Grated rind of 1 ripe lemon
1 cooked 23 cm pastry shell
    (biscuit pastry p. 91)

Meringue
2 egg whites
4 tablespoons sugar

1. Blend flour, cornflour, and sugar in a saucepan with the lemon juice.
2. Add boiling water and cook, stirring all the time until it thickens.
3. Add slightly beaten egg yolks, butter, and lemon rind. Mix well.
4. Place in cool pastry case.
5. Beat egg whites till stiff, add sugar gradually, and beat till thick.
6. Pile on top of filling. Place in oven or under a slow griller and lightly brown.

MINCE TART

$\frac{1}{3}$ cup sultanas
$\frac{1}{3}$ cup currants
$1\frac{1}{2}$ tablespoons candied peel
2 large apples
$\frac{1}{3}$ cup brown sugar
1 tablespoon butter
$\frac{1}{8}$ teaspoon nutmeg
A little grated lemon rind and juice
$\frac{1}{8}$ teaspoon spice
Double quantity shortcrust pastry (see p. 93)
Egg white or water and sugar for glazing
Icing sugar

1. Wash and dry fruit.
2. Cut peel finely.
3. Peel, quarter, and core apples; cut into dice.
4. Mix fruits, sugar, butter, and flavourings together.
5. Divide shortcrust into two, one piece a little larger than the other.
6. Roll the larger piece out a little larger than the tart-plate.
7. Line the plate with pastry.
8. Wet round the edge, and put fruit mixture in.
9. Roll out the remainder of the pastry.
10. Cover the fruit.
11. Trim pastry, firm edges together.
12. Glaze with white of egg or water and sugar.
13. Bake in a hot oven, 220°–230°C, for 15 minutes.
14. Reduce heat and cook half an hour longer.
15. Sift icing sugar over top before serving.

SMALL TARTS

Make small pastry cases using champagne or shortcrust pastry (see pp. 91, 93).

Lemon Cheese

1. Cook pastry cases. Cool.
2. Fill with lemon cheese (see p. 117).
3. Whipped cream or a small meringue may be placed on each.

Coconut

1. Place 1 teaspoon of jam in bottom of un-cooked pastry cases.
2. Mix 1 cup coconut, $\frac{1}{2}$ cup sugar.
3. Beat 1 egg and add to mixture.
4. Place spoonfuls into cases on top of jam and bake in moderate oven, 180°C, until golden brown—about 20 minutes.

Butterscotch

1. Fill uncooked pastry cases with mixture for Butterscotch Pie (see p. 96).
2. Bake at 180°C till set—about 20 minutes.
3. Top with meringue mixture.

CAKES

APPLE CAKE

Cake
½ cup butter
½ cup sugar
2 eggs (60 g)
1½ cups self-raising flour
1 cup cornflour

Apple mixture
3 apples—peeled and grated
Grated rind of 1 lemon
4 tablespoons sugar

Icing
2 cups icing sugar
Lemon juice
1 small teaspoon ground
    cinnamon

1. Have a moderate oven in readiness.
2. Grease a slab cake pan No. 28 or line with greased paper.
3. Cream butter and sugar.
4. Add well-beaten eggs.
5. Stir in lightly the sifted flour and cornflour.
6. Spread half the cake mixture in the prepared pan.
7. Cover with the apple mixture, previously prepared and mixed together.
8. Add remainder of cake mixture, spreading with knife dipped in hot water if necessary.
9. Bake in a moderate oven, 180°–190°C, for 20 to 30 minutes.
10. When cool, cover with warm icing flavoured with lemon juice.
11. Sprinkle with cinnamon.

BASIC PLAIN CAKE

½ cup margarine or butter
¾ cup sugar
4 drops vanilla essence
2 eggs
2 cups self-raising flour
½ cup milk

1. Grease and lightly flour desired pan (see step 5 below).
2. Cream margarine, sugar, and vanilla.
3. Beat eggs and add gradually, beating well after each addition. If using an electric mixer use unbeaten eggs, one at a time, and mix each one in on speed 8.
4. Add sifted flour alternately with the milk, beginning and ending with flour. Beat 1 minute on speed 4 of electric mixer, or 30 strokes with a wooden spoon.

(continued)

5. Spread in prepared pan. This quantity fills:
   a. two 18 cm shallow cake pans
   b. one 25 × 15 × 6 cm loaf cake pan
   c. two 25 × 9 × 5 cm bar cake pan
   d. one 18 × 7 cm deep cake pan
   e. one 28 × 18 × 4 cm slab cake pan
   f. one 20 × 7 cm ring pan
6. Cook on centre shelf in a moderate oven, 180°–190°C, (a), (c) and (e) 30 to 35 minutes; (b), (d) and (f) 40 to 45 minutes.
7. Test if cooked by inserting a clean thin skewer lightly into the centre of the cake. If it comes out free from mixture, the cake is cooked.
8. Stand pan on cake cooler 5 to 10 minutes before turning cake out. Cool.
9. Finish as desired.

CHOCOLATE CAKE

Use recipe for basic plain cake (p. 101) but add $\frac{1}{4}$ teaspoon bicarbonate of soda and 4 level tablespoons cocoa to the flour. Increase milk by one tablespoon.

ORANGE CAKE

Use recipe for basic plain cake (p.101) but add 2 teaspoons grated orange rind to sifted flour. Decrease milk by 3 tablespoons. Add 3 tablespoons orange juice separately from the milk.

COCONUT CAKE

Use recipe for basic plain cake (p.101) but add $\frac{1}{2}$ cup desiccated coconut before the flour and milk.

APPLE CAKE

Use recipe for basic plain cake (p. 101) but use a ring cake pan. Top batter with very thin slices of peeled apples. Sprinkle with 2 teaspoons sugar and $\frac{1}{2}$ teaspoon cinnamon mixed together.

PATTY CAKES

Use recipe for basic plain cakes (p. 101) but spoon into 24 greased patty pans.

SPICE CAKE

Use recipe for basic plain cake (p. 101) but add 1 teaspoon ginger, $\frac{1}{2}$ teaspoon cinnamon, and $\frac{1}{2}$ teaspoon nutmeg to flour. Decrease sugar to 1 cup and add $\frac{1}{2}$ cup brown sugar.

MARBLE CAKE

Use recipe for basic plain cake (p. 101) but divide batter into three in separate bowls. Leave one plain. Add red food colour to another. Add 2 tablespoons cocoa, $\frac{1}{8}$ teaspoon bicarbonate of soda and 1 tablespoon milk to the third. Drop in alternate colours into the prepared pan until all batter is used. Draw a thick skewer or thin bladed knife in circles through the batter to streak the colours.

CHERRY CAKE

Use recipe for basic plain cake (p. 101) but add 1 cup drained cherries cut into large pieces before adding flour. Almond essence may be used instead of vanilla.

SEED CAKE

Use recipe for basic plain cake (p. 101) but add 1 tablespoon caraway seeds before the flour.

CHEESE CAKES

1 quantity shortcrust pastry
(see p. 93)
Jam
1 quantity plain cake mixture
(see p. 101)

1. Attend to oven.
2. Roll pastry out thinly and stamp into rounds with a fancy cutter.
3. Line patty pans with pastry rounds.
4. Put $\frac{1}{2}$ teaspoon of jam in each.
5. Put a teaspoon of cake mixture into each prepared patty pan.
6. Decorate tops with strips of pastry in fancy shapes made from scraps.
7. Bake in a hot oven, 230°–250°C, for 20 minutes, gradually decreasing heat.
8. Turn onto a cake cooler to cool.

CHOCOLATE ECLAIRS

1 quantity choux pastry mixture (see p. 91)
1 bottle cream (250 g)
1 quantity chocolate icing (see p. 116)

1. Force pastry mixture through bag and plain pipe in 5 cm lengths onto greased pan.
2. Bake in a moderately hot oven, 200°–230°C, for $\frac{1}{2}$ hour. Do not open oven door for at least 10 minutes.
3. When cool make an incision in one side and fill with sweetened and flavoured whipped cream.
4. Cover with chocolate icing.

CHRISTMAS CAKE

250 g (1 cup) butter
1 cup sugar
6 eggs (60 g)

1. Attend to oven.
2. Line an 18 × 7 cm deep cake pan with 2 or 3 folds of paper or with aluminium foil.

(continued)

$1\frac{1}{2}$ cups sultanas
$1\frac{1}{2}$ cups currants
1 teaspoon caramel
$1\frac{1}{2}$ cups raisins
$1\frac{1}{2}$ cups citron peel
3 tablespoons dates or figs (chopped)
3 tablespoons almonds
$2\frac{1}{2}$ cups plain flour
$\frac{1}{2}$ cup brandy or sherry

3. Beat butter and sugar to a cream, and add caramel.
4. Add the beaten eggs, one at a time, and continue beating.
5. Add the prepared fruit and nuts.
6. Add flour, and lastly brandy or sherry, mixing well.
7. Pour into prepared pan.
8. Bake in slow oven, 140°–150°C, for 3 to $3\frac{1}{2}$ hours.
9. Test by piercing with a skewer. If it is free from mixture when withdrawn, the cake is cooked.
10. Allow to remain in pan till cold.

CINNAMON CRUMBLE RING

2 cups self-raising flour
2 tablespoons sugar
1 egg
1 cup milk
3 tablespoons margarine
Topping
3 tablespoons self-raising flour
3 tablespoons brown sugar
1 tablespoon margarine

1. Sift flour; stir in sugar.
2. Beat egg, add milk.
3. Melt margarine.
4. Make a well in centre of flour and sugar and beat in egg and milk mixture.
5. Add melted margarine and mix well.
6. Pour into a well-greased 20 × 7 cm ring cake pan.
7. Mix all ingredients for topping together.
8. Sprinkle over cake.
9. Bake at 180°–200°C for about 30 minutes.

CREAM OR CUSTARD PUFFS

1 quantity choux pastry (see p. 91)
Cream or custard (see overleaf)
Icing sugar

1. Grease scone tray.
2. Place small spoonfuls of pastry onto pan, allowing room to spread.
3. Bake in a hot oven, 220°–250°C, for $\frac{1}{2}$ hour or longer, gradually decreasing heat. Do not open oven door for at least 10 minutes.
4. When cooked, cool on a cooler.
5. When cool, open near the top.
6. Fill with whipped cream or custard.
7. Sprinkle with icing sugar.

CUSTARD FOR PUFFS

2 tablespoons butter
2 tablespoons plain flour
$1\frac{1}{4}$ cups milk
2 egg yolks (60 g)
$1\frac{1}{2}$ tablespoons sugar
Vanilla to taste

1. Melt butter.
2. Add flour and beat smooth.
3. Cook well for 2 minutes.
4. Add milk; stir until boiling.
5. Remove from heat.
6. Beat and add egg yolks.
7. Add sugar.
8. Return to heat and cook for a minute without boiling, stirring continually.
9. Add vanilla.
10. Cool before using for filling.

FRUIT CAKE

4 cups plain flour
1 teaspoon spice
250 g (1 cup) butter
$1\frac{1}{2}$ cups brown sugar
3 cups sultanas
3 cups raisins
$\frac{3}{4}$ cup peel
2 eggs (60 g)
$1\frac{1}{2}$ teaspoons bicarbonate of soda
1 cup boiling milk

1. Have moderate oven in readiness.
2. Prepare a 20 × 7 cm deep cake pan, lining with paper.
3. Sift flour and spice, and rub in the butter.
4. Add sugar, sultanas, raisins, and finely cut peel, and mix well together.
5. Stir in lightly the well-beaten eggs.
6. Dissolve bicarbonate of soda in the boiling milk (heated in large vessel) and pour at once onto the other ingredients.
7. Mix well together.
8. Place in prepared pan and bake at 160°–180°C for 2 to 3 hours according to size of cake.

Note. Brandy may be used in this recipe, the quantity of milk being reduced accordingly.

GINGER SPONGE

1 tablespoon butter
$\frac{1}{2}$ cup brown sugar
1 egg (60 g)
$\frac{1}{2}$ cup milk
1 tablespoon treacle or golden syrup

1. Attend to oven.
2. Grease two 18 × 4 cm shallow cake pans.
3. Beat butter and sugar to a cream.
4. Beat egg well, mix the milk and treacle with it.

(continued)

1 cup plain flour
2 teaspoons ginger
2 teaspoons cinnamon
1 teaspoon bicarbonate of soda
Mock cream (see p.117)
Icing sugar

5. Add gradually to the creamed butter and sugar.
6. Stir in the sifted flour, ginger, cinnamon, and soda lightly.
7. Pour into the prepared pans.
8. Bake at 150°–180°C for about 15 minutes.
9. Turn onto a cooler to cool.
10. When cool join together with mock cream and sprinkle with icing sugar.

GINGERBREAD

1½ cups plain flour
1 teaspoon bicarbonate of soda
2 tablespoons margarine or clarified fat
¼ cup brown sugar
2 tablespoons finely chopped candied peel (optional)
1 egg (60 g)
2 tablespoons treacle or golden syrup
½ cup warm milk
2 teaspoons ground ginger
¼ teaspoon cinnamon or spice

1. Attend to oven.
2. Grease and line a 28 × 18 × 4 cm slab cake pan with greaseproof paper.
3. Sift flour and bicarbonate of soda.
4. Rub in fat with tips of fingers.
5. Add sugar and candied peel.
6. Beat egg; add to it treacle and milk, and mix well.
7. Pour into dry ingredients, mix well, and bake in a very moderate oven, 150°–180°C, about 20 to 30 minutes.

KISS CAKES

60 g (¼ cup) butter
¼ cup sugar
1 egg (60 g)
½ cup plain flour
½ cup cornflour
1 teaspoon baking powder
Jam
Icing sugar

1. Attend to oven.
2. Grease an oven slide.
3. Beat butter and sugar to a cream.
4. Add well-beaten egg.
5. Add sifted flour, cornflour, and baking powder.
6. Stir lightly, adding extra flour if necessary to make a stiff dough.
7. Put half-teaspoonfuls of mixture on oven slide, 2 cm apart.
8. Bake at 160°–180°C for about 8 minutes.
9. Turn onto a cooler.
10. When cool, join together with jam and sprinkle with icing sugar.

LEMON TEACAKE

125 g ($\frac{1}{2}$ cup) butter or margarine
$\frac{3}{4}$ cup castor sugar
1 egg (60 g)
1$\frac{3}{4}$ cups self-raising flour
$\frac{1}{2}$ cup milk
2 teaspoons of finely grated lemon rind
Extra $\frac{1}{4}$ cup sugar
$\frac{1}{4}$ cup lemon juice

1. Grease a 25 × 15 × 6 cm loaf cake pan.
2. Cream butter and sugar.
3. Beat egg, add slowly to creamed mixture and beat well.
4. Sift flour.
5. Add alternately with milk, stirring well.
6. Fold in lemon rind.
7. Place in prepared pan.
8. Bake in a moderate oven, 180°–190°C, for 30 to 35 minutes.
9. Dissolve extra sugar in lemon juice, stand in warm place.
10. When cake is cooked, remove from oven and gently spoon lemon and sugar over top.
11. Allow to remain in pan till cool.

Note. Orange rind may be used instead of lemon.

MERINGUES

3 egg whites (60 g)
Pinch salt
$\frac{1}{2}$ cup crystal sugar
Scant $\frac{1}{2}$ cup castor sugar

1. Slightly damp greaseproof paper or aluminium foil on a flat baking tray.
2. Beat whites of eggs with salt till frothy and stiff.
3. Add crystal sugar and beat till thick.
4. Fold in castor sugar.
5. Place in small spoonfuls on prepared tray 2 cm apart.
6. Bake in a slow oven, 120°–140°C, for 1 to 1$\frac{1}{2}$ hours, until dry.

ECONOMICAL MERINGUE SHELL

1 egg white (60 g)
1 cup castor sugar
2 tablespoons boiling water
$\frac{1}{2}$ teaspoon vanilla
1 teaspoon vinegar
1 teaspoon baking powder

1. Beat egg white till stiff.
2. Add sugar and beat till disolved.
3. Add boiling water all at once and continue beating until the mixture will stand in peaks.

(continued)

Gingerbread (p. 107), Meringues (p. 108), and Swiss Roll (p. 114).

4. Add vanilla and vinegar, and lastly fold in baking powder.
5. Pile onto well-greased paper.
6. Bake in a slow oven, 100°–120°C, for $1\frac{1}{2}$ hours.

Note. This mixture may be made into small meringues by placing spoonfuls onto greased paper. Bake as above until dry and firm.

PAVLOVA

4 egg whites (60 g)
1 cup castor sugar
$\frac{1}{2}$ tablespoon cornflour
1 teaspoon vinegar or lemon juice

1. Lightly damp greaseproof paper or aluminium foil cut to size and shape of pavlova.
2. Beat egg whites till stiff and frothy.
3. Gradually add sugar and beat till thick.
4. Fold in sifted cornflour and vinegar or lemon juice.
5. Spread with spoon or pipe onto the prepared paper.
6. Bake in slow oven, 120°–150°C, for 2 hours.

PIKELETS

1 egg (60 g)
4 tablespoons sugar
1 cup self-raising flour
$\frac{3}{4}$ cup milk
$\frac{1}{4}$ teaspoon bicarbonate of soda
1 tablespoon melted butter

1. Beat egg and sugar.
2. Add flour alternately with milk in which bicarbonate of soda has been dissolved.
3. Add melted butter.
4. Have ready a hot greased pan or griddle iron.
5. Put mixture in dessertspoonfuls in pan or on griddle iron.
6. Brown both sides, lift out, and drain on absorbent paper.

Assorted Biscuits (pp. 119–120), Shortbread (p. 126).

PLAIN CAKES

$\frac{1}{4}$ cup butter or margarine
$\frac{1}{4}$ cup sugar
1 egg
4 tablespoons milk
Vanilla to taste
1 cup self-raising flour

1. Attend to oven.
2. Grease 12-hole deep patty pans with butter.
3. Beat butter and sugar to a cream.
4. Add well-beaten egg gradually.
5. Add milk and vanilla alternately with sifted flour, stir in lightly.
6. Place mixture into patty pans.
7. Bake in oven 200°–230°C about 10 minutes.
8. Turn on a cooler to cool.

RAINBOW CAKE

1 cup butter or margarine
1 cup sugar
3 eggs (60 g)
$\frac{1}{2}$ cup milk
Vanilla essence to taste
3 cups plain flour
2 teaspoons baking powder
A few drops red colouring
2 tablespoons cocoa
Jam
Icing sugar
(Self-raising flour may be used instead of plain flour and baking powder)

1. Attend to oven.
2. Grease three 18 × 4 cm shallow pans well with butter.
3. Beat butter and sugar until creamy.
4. Add well-beaten eggs; beat well.
5. Add milk and essence alternatively with sifted flour and baking powder, mixing quickly and lightly, but do not beat.
6. Divide mixture into 3 equal parts.
7. Colour one part pink with red colouring; add cocoa to another part; leave the third part plain.
8. Pour each part into a different pan; smooth over with a knife.
9. Cook in a moderate oven, 180°–190°C, for about 20 to 30 minutes.
10. Turn on a cooler to cool.
11. Join together with jam; sprinkle with icing sugar.

RASPBERRY BUNS

2 cups self-raising flour
2 tablespoons butter or mar-
    garine
$\frac{1}{4}$ cup sugar
1 egg
4 tablespoons milk
Raspberry jam
Pinch salt

1. Attend to oven.
2. Grease an oven slide.
3. Sift flour and salt.
4. Rub butter in lightly.
5. Add sugar, free from lumps.
6. Beat egg, add to it the milk.
7. Pour egg and milk into dry ingredients.
8. Mix into a light dough.
9. Turn onto a slightly floured board.
10. Divide into 12 parts.
11. Knead each one lightly round.
12. Make a hollow in the centre of each.
13. Put in a little jam.
14. Pinch together, enclosing jam.
15. Glaze with a little milk.
16. Bake on the oven slide, 200°–230°C, for 15 minutes.

ROCK CAKES

2 cups self-raising flour
$\frac{1}{3}$ cup butter or margarine
$\frac{1}{2}$ cup sugar
$\frac{1}{2}$ teaspoon ground ginger
2 tablespoons currants, sul-
    tanas, chopped dates, or
    mixed fruit
1 egg (60 g)
3 tablespoons milk

1. Attend to oven.
2. Grease an oven slide.
3. Sift flour.
4. Rub in butter lightly with tips of fingers.
5. Add sugar and ginger.
6. Add currants or sultanas, washed and dried, or chopped dates.
7. Beat egg, and add to it the milk.
8. Add egg and milk to dry ingredients, and make into a stiff dough.
9. Place mixture in small, rough heaps on prepared oven slide.
10. Bake in a hot oven, 200°–230°C, for 10 to 15 minutes.
11. Allow to cool on a cake cooler.

SPONGE SANDWICH (1)

3 eggs
$\frac{3}{4}$ cup sugar
1 cup plain flour
2 teaspoons baking powder
3 tablespoons water
Jam or other filling
Icing sugar
(Self-raising flour may be used instead of plain flour and baking powder)

1. Attend to oven.
2. Grease two 18 × 4 cm shallow cake pans.
3. Separate egg whites from yolks.
4. Beat whites till stiff; add sugar slowly and beat well.
5. Add yolks and beat till thick.
6. Fold in sifted flour and baking powder.
7. Add water; stir lightly and quickly.
8. Pour into pans.
9. Bake in a moderate oven, 180°–190° C, for 10 to 15 minutes.
10. Turn onto a cake cooler or paper sprinkled with icing sugar.
11. When cool, join together with jam or suitable filling and sprinkle with icing sugar.

SPONGE SANDWICH (2)

2 eggs
$\frac{1}{2}$ cup sugar
$\frac{1}{2}$ teaspoon bicarbonate of soda
1 tablespoon melted butter
3 tablespoons hot water
1 cup plain flour
1 teaspoon cream of tartar
Jam or cream
Icing sugar

1. Grease two 15 × 4 cm shallow cake pans.
2. Separate egg whites and yolks.
3. Beat whites till stiff, add sugar and beat well.
4. Add yolks and continue beating until thick.
5. Dissolve bicarbonate of soda and butter in hot water.
6. Add the sifted flour and cream of tartar to eggs and stir lightly.
7. Add butter, water, and soda; mix or fold lightly and quickly, stirring as little as possible.
8. Pour into pans and bake in a very moderate oven, 180°–190° C, for about 10 to 15 minutes.
9. Turn onto a cooler.
10. Join together with jam or cream filling.
11. Sprinkle with sifted icing sugar.

Note. This mixture is suitable only for small shallow pans or a recess pan.

LARGE SPONGE CAKE

6 eggs (60 g)
1 cup sugar
$\frac{1}{4}$ cup water
A few drops of vanilla essence
2 cups plain flour
Pinch salt

1. Attend to oven.
2. Grease a 23 × 8 cm deep cake pan, then sprinkle it with sifted sugar and flour; shake well.
3. Break eggs into a large basin.
4. Put sugar and water into an enamelled saucepan; when dissolved, bring to the boil and boil 1 minute.
5. Pour slowly onto eggs, then beat well until thick, about $\frac{1}{2}$ an hour if beaten by hand.
6. Add vanilla.
7. Stir in sifted flour and salt.
8. Mix quickly and lightly and pour into cake pan.
9. Bake slowly, 150°–160°C, for 1 hour.
10. Stand pan on a cake cooler for five minutes before turning cake onto cooler.

SULTANA CAKE

250 g (1 cup) butter
1 cup sugar
3 eggs
$\frac{2}{3}$ cup milk
$1\frac{1}{2}$ cups sultanas
3 tablespoons almonds
3 tablespoons peel
3 cups plain flour
$1\frac{1}{2}$ teaspoons baking powder

1. Attend to oven.
2. Grease an 18 × 7 cm deep cake pan with butter.
3. Beat butter and sugar to a cream.
4. Add eggs, well-beaten.
5. Add milk gradually.
6. Add cleaned sultanas, blanched and chopped almonds, and finely-sliced peel.
7. Add sifted flour and baking powder.
8. Stir lightly until well mixed.
9. Pour into the cake pan.
10. Bake at 160°–180°C for about $1\frac{1}{2}$ hours.
11. Turn onto cooler to cool.

SWISS ROLL

3 eggs (60 g)
$\frac{1}{2}$ cup sugar
1 cup plain flour
$\frac{1}{2}$ teaspoon bicarbonate of soda and 1 teaspoon cream of tartar, or 2 teaspoons baking powder
2 tablespoons hot milk
3 tablespoons jam

1. Attend to oven.
2. Grease 35 × 25 × 2 cm Swiss roll pan and line with greased paper.
3. Beat egg whites and yolks separately, whites until stiff, then together.
4. Add sugar, and continue beating until thick.
5. Stir in sifted flour, cream of tartar and bicarbonate of soda *or* baking powder, mixing very lightly.
6. Heat milk and add to mixture, stirring lightly.
7. Pour mixture into lined pan.
8. Bake in a moderate oven, 190°–200°C, for about 10 minutes.
9. Turn onto a sugared paper.
10. Roll up.
11. Unroll.
12. Spread quickly with jam.
13. Roll up, and place on a cooler to cool.

ICING AND FILLINGS
FOR CAKES

ALMOND PASTE ICING

$1\frac{1}{3}$ cups icing sugar or castor
    sugar
1 cup ground almonds
1 egg yolk
1 tablespoon sherry or orange
    or lemon juice

1. Sift sugar.
2. Add almonds, and mix well.
3. Mix into a very stiff paste with beaten yolk of egg and sherry or fruit juice.
4. Lift out onto board which has been sprinkled with icing sugar.
5. Roll out and cover cake.

Note. Cake should be brushed with egg white before covering.

BOILED ICING

2 tablespoons water
1 cup white sugar
1 egg white
Vanilla essence to taste
Colouring

1. Put water and sugar in a saucepan and boil gently for 5 minutes without stirring.
2. Beat egg white to a stiff froth in a basin.
3. Pour on the boiling syrup gradually, and beat until thick.
4. Add vanilla, and, if liked, a little colouring.
5. Pour over cake.

CARAMEL ICING

2 cups brown sugar
$\frac{1}{2}$ cup milk
2 tablespoons butter
$\frac{1}{4}$ teaspoon vanilla

1. Place sugar, milk, and butter in a saucepan.
2. Stir over heat till boiling.
3. Boil without stirring for five minutes.
4. Remove from heat. Add vanilla.
5. Stir till consistency of honey and pour over cake.

CHOCOLATE ICING

1 cup icing sugar
2 tablespoons powdered chocolate or cocoa
2 tablespoons boiling water

1. Sift icing sugar, and add chocolate.
2. Place in a clean saucepan and gradually add boiling water.
3. Stir over heat until warm and smooth.
4. Pour over cake.

ORANGE OR FRUIT ICING

1 cup icing sugar
2 tablespoons fruit juice

1. Sift icing sugar.
2. Place in saucepan with fruit juice, and stir over heat until just warm.
3. Pour over cake, smooth with a knife dipped in hot water if necessary.

Note. Passionfruit juice may be strained or a few seeds left in as desired. Grated rind of orange may be added to orange icing.

ROYAL ICING

500 g pure icing sugar
2 egg whites (60 g)
$\frac{1}{4}$ teaspoon lemon juice
1 teaspoon glucose

1. Sift icing sugar.
2. Place the egg whites in a basin with lemon juice and glucose.
3. Work the icing sugar gradually into the other ingredients until the desired consistency.

WARM ICING

1 cup icing sugar
1 tablespoon boiling water
Essence to taste
Colouring

1. Sift the icing sugar.
2. Add boiling water gradually, and mix to a thick paste. Do not add all water unless necessary.
3. Stir over boiling water until smooth consistency.
4. Add essence and colouring if required.
5. Place on cake; smooth with a knife.

CREAM FILLING FOR CAKES

$\frac{2}{3}$ cup cream
1 tablespoon sugar
1 egg white
Juice of 3 passionfruit

1. Whip cream with the sugar till thick.
2. Beat the egg white till very stiff.
3. Add beaten white to fruit pulp.
4. Work the cream in slowly.
5. Spread between layers of cake.

Note. Chopped almonds or walnuts may be used instead of passionfruit.

LEMON CHEESE

1 lemon
1 egg yolk
$\frac{1}{4}$ cup sugar
$1\frac{1}{2}$ tablespoons butter

1. Put the grated rind and juice of the lemon into a saucepan.
2. Add the egg yolk, sugar, and butter, and stir over heat till thick.
3. Allow to cool.
4. Spread between layers of cake.

Note. The whole egg may be beaten and used if liked.

LEMON OR ORANGE FILLING FOR CAKES

2 tablespoons arrowroot
$\frac{2}{3}$ cup water
1 tablespoon butter
1 tablespoon sugar
1 teaspoon grated lemon or orange rind
2 tablespoons lemon or orange juice

1. Blend arrowroot with a little water.
2. Boil water and butter; add moistened arrowroot; stir and cook for 3 minutes.
3. Add sugar and grated rind and juice of fruit.
4. When cool, spread between layers of cake.

MOCK CREAM FILLING (1)

2 tablespoons butter
$\frac{1}{2}$ cup sifted icing sugar
$\frac{1}{2}$ teaspoon vanilla essence

1. Beat butter and icing sugar to a cream.
2. Add vanilla; stir in well.
3. Spread between layers of cake.

MOCK CREAM FILLING (2)

1 tablespoon maize cornflour
$\frac{1}{2}$ cup milk
3 tablespoons butter
2 tablespoons castor sugar
$\frac{1}{2}$ teaspoon vanilla essence

1. Moisten the cornflour with a little of the milk.
2. Put the remainder of milk on to boil.
3. Stir in moistened cornflour and cook 2 minutes.
4. Lift off and allow to cool.
5. Beat butter and sugar to a cream.
6. Add vanilla.
7. Gradually stir in the thickened milk.
8. Beat well.
9. Use as a filling for cakes.

BISCUITS AND SLICES

To keep biscuits crisp they should be stored in *airtight* containers as soon as they are cold. Different varieties should be stored separately.

ANZAC BISCUITS

1 cup rolled oats
1 cup plain flour
$\frac{1}{3}$ cup sugar
$\frac{3}{4}$ cup desiccated coconut
2 tablespoons golden syrup
$\frac{1}{2}$ cup butter or margarine
$\frac{1}{2}$ teaspoon bicarbonate of soda
1 tablespoon boiling water
Pinch salt

1. Mix oats, flour, sugar, and coconut together.
2. Melt syrup and butter together.
3. Mix soda with boiling water and add to melted butter and syrup.
4. Add to dry ingredients.
5. Place tablespoonfuls of mixture on greased slide.
6. Bake in slow oven, 150°–160°C, for 20 minutes.

BASIC BISCUIT RECIPE (1)—VANILLA BISCUITS

$\frac{1}{2}$ cup butter or margarine
$\frac{1}{2}$ cup sugar
$\frac{1}{4}$ teaspoon vanilla
1 egg (60 g)
2 cups plain flour
1 teaspoon baking powder
Egg or milk for glazing
Cherries and almonds
Pinch salt

1. Grease pan or slide.
2. Cream butter, sugar, and vanilla.
3. Beat egg and add slowly to mixture, beating well.
4. Add sifted flour and baking powder.
5. Place onto floured board, knead lightly.
6. Roll out part of the mixture at a time, keeping remainder cool.
7. Stamp out shapes with a cutter dipped in flour.
8. Put onto greased pan or slide.
9. Glaze with a little egg or milk.
10. Place a piece of cherry or almond on each.
11. Bake in very moderate oven, 150°–160°C, for about 10 minutes. The biscuits should be a very light brown when cooked.

(continued)

12. Allow to cool on slide.

Note. To make a variety of biscuits from this mixture, use half as above, and prepare the other half as follows:

Mix a small portion with chopped cherries, roll into balls and press onto greased tray.
Roll the remainder into balls, press with a fork on greased tray, and top with pieces of ginger, grated chocolate, or chocolate pieces.

BASIC BISCUIT RECIPE (2)

$1\frac{1}{2}$ cups self-raising flour
Pinch salt
$\frac{1}{2}$ cup custard powder
$\frac{1}{2}$ cup sugar
$\frac{1}{2}$ cup margarine or butter
3 tablespoons milk

1. Grease and flour two oven slides.
2. Sift flour, salt, and custard powder into bowl.
3. Add sugar.
4. Add margarine and rub in with tips of fingers until the mixture is like coarse breadcrumbs.
5. Add milk and mix very firmly by hand (a little extra milk is sometimes needed in cold weather).
6. Turn onto floured board and roll round with hand to coat lightly with flour.
7. Roll out thinly with floured rolling pin.
8. Cut into desired shapes (if a 4 cm round cutter is used, this amount makes about 4 dozen biscuits).
9. Cook on prepared slides in a moderate oven, $150°-180°C$, for 12 to 15 minutes. Place one slide above the centre and one on centre rack of oven.
10. Remove from slides with a knife while hot, as the biscuits are inclined to stick if left until cold.

CHOCOLATE COOKIES

Use basic biscuit recipe (2) but add 2 tablespoons cocoa to flour, *or* add 60g chocolate pieces, and drop dough in rough heaps. An extra teaspoon of milk may be necessary.

CHERRY AND NUT DROPS

Use basic biscuit recipe (2) but add 60 g chopped cherries and 60 g chopped walnuts or peanuts. Drop in rough heaps without rolling.

COCONUT ROUGHS

Use basic biscuit recipe (2) but add ½ cup desiccated coconut. Drop in rough heaps.

SPICY DATE DROPS

Use basic biscuit recipe (2) but add ½ teaspoon cinnamon, ¼ teaspoon nutmeg, and ½ cup chopped dates. Drop in rough heaps.

CARAMEL FINGERS

½ cup butter or margarine
¾ cup brown sugar
¼ cup chopped dates
1 egg
½ cup chopped walnuts
1 cup self-raising flour
Pinch salt

1. Grease a 28 × 18 × 4 cm slab cake pan.
2. Melt butter and sugar over slow heat.
3. Beat well and allow to cool.
4. Beat egg and add to butter and sugar.
5. Add dates, nuts, and lastly flour. Beat till smooth.
6. Press into pan.
7. Bake in moderate oven, 160°–190° C, for 20 to 30 minutes.
8. Cool in pan.
9. Cut into finger lengths.

CHEESE STRAWS OR BISCUITS

¾ cup dry cheese
¼ cup butter or margarine
¾ cup plain flour
Salt and cayenne pepper to taste
1 egg yolk
½ teaspoon lemon juice

1. Grate cheese.
2. Mix butter lightly into flour.
3. Add cheese, salt, and cayenne.
4. Mix egg yolk and lemon juice, add to flour mixture, and mix to a stiff dough.
5. Roll out part of dough 5 mm thick.

(continued)

6. Cut into strips 10 cm long and 5 mm wide.
7. Roll out remainder of dough, stamp into rounds with a plain cutter, and cut out centre with a smaller cutter leaving a ring.
8. Bake on greased slide in a moderate oven, 150°–160°C, for 10 to 20 minutes.
9. Cool on slide.
10. To serve, fill each ring with a bundle of straws. Arrange on plate. Garnish with parsley.

Note. This mixture may be used for biscuits. Cut with a floured cutter instead of making strips and rings.

CHOCOLATE BISCUITS

$\frac{1}{2}$ cup butter or margarine
$\frac{1}{2}$ cup sugar
2 tablespoons condensed milk
Vanilla to taste
1 cup self-raising flour
$\frac{1}{2}$ cup chocolate (grated or chopped)

1. Cream butter and sugar.
2. Add condensed milk and vanilla. Beat well.
3. Add flour and lastly chocolate.
4. Place in small spoonfuls on a greased slide.
5. Bake at 150°–180°C for 10 to 15 minutes.

CHOCOLATE COCONUT SLICE

$\frac{1}{4}$ cup butter or margarine
$\frac{3}{4}$ cup brown sugar
1 egg (55 g or 60 g)
1 cup self-raising flour
$\frac{1}{2}$ cup desiccated coconut
Pinch salt

1. Melt butter and sugar. Cool.
2. Beat in egg.
3. Sift and add flour, then coconut. Mix thoroughly.
4. Press into a greased shallow pan 23 cm square.
5. Bake at 150°–180°C for 20 to 25 minutes.
6. Mark into slices and leave in pan till cold. It may be iced with chocolate icing if desired.

CHOCOLATE FUDGE FINGERS

$\frac{1}{2}$ cup butter or margarine
1 cup brown sugar
3 tablespoons cocoa or pow-
    dered chocolate
1 egg (60 g)
250 g plain sweet biscuits
1 cup mixed fruit or crushed
    nuts

1. Place butter, sugar, and cocoa in saucepan.
2. Stir over slow heat till butter melts and all three ingredients are thoroughly mixed.
3. Allow to cool.
4. Beat egg.
5. Crush biscuits to fine crumb.
6. Add egg, crushed biscuits, and fruit or nuts to cooled mixture.
7. Mix well, spread into a greased 20 cm slab cake pan, and place in refrigerator to set.
8. Cut into fingers.

CINNAMON DROPS

$1\frac{1}{2}$ cups plain flour
$1\frac{1}{2}$ teaspoons baking powder
3 teaspoons cinnamon
Little grated nutmeg
$\frac{1}{2}$ cup butter or margarine
$\frac{1}{2}$ cup sugar
1 egg (60 g)
1 tablespoon milk
12 almonds, blanched and split

1. Sift flour, baking powder, cinnamon, and nutmeg.
2. Rub in butter or margarine lightly.
3. Add sugar.
4. Add well-beaten egg and milk, keeping a little for glazing.
5. Shape into small balls, rolling lightly in palms of hands.
6. Put on greased slides, brush over top with little egg.
7. Put small piece of almond on top of each.
8. Bake in moderate oven, $150°–180°$C, about 10 minutes.

CORNFLAKE CRISPS

2 egg whites (60 g eggs)
$\frac{1}{2}$ cup sugar
4 cups cornflakes
$\frac{3}{4}$ cup chopped nuts
$\frac{1}{2}$ cup desiccated coconut
2 tablespoons melted butter
Pinch salt

1. Beat egg whites, add sugar, and beat till stiff.
2. Add dry ingredients.
3. Lastly add melted butter.
4. Place in spoonfuls on a greased slide.
5. Bake in moderate oven, $150°–160°$C, for 10 to 15 minutes.

GINGER BISCUITS

$\frac{1}{2}$ cup margarine or butter
3 tablespoons golden syrup
3 cups self-raising flour
1 teaspoon bicarbonate of soda
1 tablespoon ground ginger
1 cup sugar
1 egg
Pinch salt

1. Melt margarine with golden syrup on gentle heat. Cool.
2. Sift flour, bicarbonate of soda, and ginger, and add sugar.
3. Beat egg and stir into margarine and syrup.
4. Add dry ingredients and mix well together.
5. Roll into balls and place on a greased slide.
6. Cook in a very moderate oven, 150°–180°C, for approximately 20 minutes.

GINGER OR FRUIT SLICE

$\frac{1}{2}$ cup margarine or butter
$\frac{1}{2}$ cup brown sugar
1 teaspoon grated lemon rind
1 tablespoon golden syrup
1 egg
$1\frac{1}{2}$ cups self-raising flour
1 teaspoon ground ginger
$\frac{2}{3}$ cup chopped ginger or crystallized pineapple and cherries

1. Cream margarine and sugar, lemon rind, and syrup.
2. Beat egg and add gradually.
3. Stir in sifted flour and ground ginger and chopped ginger or fruit.
4. Spread over the base of a well-greased 28 × 18 × 4 cm shallow slab cake pan.
5. Bake in moderate oven, 180°–200°C, for 40 to 45 minutes.
6. Cool in pan.
7. Ice with lemon icing, if liked.

MARSHMALLOW BISCUITS

$\frac{1}{3}$ cup butter
$\frac{1}{2}$ cup sugar
1 egg
1 cup self-raising flour
Topping
$\frac{1}{2}$ tablespoon gelatine
$\frac{1}{4}$ cup cold water
2 tablespoons boiling water
1 cup sugar
Grated chocolate or toasted coconut

1. Cream butter and sugar.
2. Add egg and beat well.
3. Sift flour and stir into creamed mixture.
4. Press into a well-greased 35 × 25 × 2 cm Swiss roll pan.
5. Bake at 160°–190°C for 10 to 20 minutes.
6. Place gelatine in saucepan with cold water, add boiling water and dissolve gelatine.
7. Add sugar and bring to boiling point.
8. Remove from heat, beat till stiff.
9. Pour over the biscuit.
10. Sprinkle with grated chocolate or toasted coconut.

MELTING MOMENTS

$\frac{1}{2}$ cup butter or margarine
2 tablespoons icing sugar
Vanilla to taste
$\frac{1}{2}$ cup self-raising flour
$\frac{1}{2}$ cup cornflour
Icing
1 tablespoon butter
1 tablespoon condensed milk
3 tablespoons icing sugar
Vanilla to taste

1. Cream butter and sugar and vanilla.
2. Sift self-raising flour and cornflour.
3. Add to creamed mixture and mix well.
4. Roll into small balls.
5. Place on greased flat pan.
6. Bake in slow oven, 150°–160°C, for 10 to 15 minutes.
7. Mix all icing ingredients together.
8. Join biscuits together with icing when cold.

NUTTIES

250 g butter or margarine
1 cup sugar
1 egg
$\frac{3}{4}$ cup dates
Pinch salt
$\frac{3}{4}$ cup walnuts
2 cups plain flour
2 teaspoons cinnamon
$\frac{1}{2}$ teaspoon bicarbonate of soda

1. Cream butter and sugar.
2. Add beaten egg.
3. Add chopped dates and walnuts.
4. Add flour and cinnamon.
5. Add bicarbonate of soda dissolved in 1 teaspoon water. Mix well.
6. Place in rough pieces on greased slides.
7. Bake at 150°–160°C for 20 minutes.

PEANUT BISCUITS

$\frac{1}{2}$ cup butter or margarine
$\frac{1}{2}$ cup sugar
1 egg
$1\frac{1}{4}$ cups self-raising flour
$\frac{3}{4}$ cup raw peanuts
Pinch salt

1. Cream butter and sugar.
2. Add egg and beat well.
3. Mix in sifted flour and peanuts.
4. Place in small portions on a greased tray.
5. Bake at 160°–190°C for 12 to 15 minutes.

Note. For a chocolate flavour, add 2 tablespoons cocoa to above mixture.

RASPBERRY SLICES

$\frac{1}{2}$ cup butter
$\frac{1}{2}$ cup sugar
2 eggs (60 g each)
1$\frac{1}{2}$ cups self-raising flour
Raspberry jam
$\frac{1}{2}$ cup additional sugar
1 cup desiccated coconut
Pinch salt

1. Cream butter and sugar together.
2. Add 1 egg.
3. Add sifted flour. Mix well.
4. Spread thinly in flat well greased or lined 35 × 25 × 2 cm Swiss roll pan.
5. Spread with raspberry jam.
6. Beat remaining egg and sugar together, add coconut.
7. Spread over jam.
8. Bake in a moderate oven, 180°–200°C, for about 20 minutes.
9. When cold cut into slices.

REFRIGERATOR BISCUITS

3 cups plain flour
1$\frac{1}{2}$ teaspoons baking powder
$\frac{2}{3}$ cup butter or margarine
1$\frac{1}{4}$ cups brown sugar
1 teaspoon vanilla essence
1 egg (60 g)
$\frac{1}{2}$ cup finely chopped dates
$\frac{1}{2}$ cup chopped cherries
$\frac{1}{2}$ cup chopped raisins or ginger or nuts
Pinch salt

1. Sift flour and baking powder.
2. Cream butter, sugar and vanilla.
3. Beat egg and add to creamed mixture.
4. Add flour and mix well.
5. Divide into four equal parts. Make one section into a roll about 4 cm in diameter. Knead dates into second section and roll as above. Knead cherries into third section and roll. Knead raisins or ginger or nuts into fourth section and roll.
6. Wrap each section in plastic wrap or waxed paper.
7. Chill in refrigerator until quite firm.
8. Slice thinly. Place onto a greased slide.
9. Bake at 150°–180°C for 10 to 15 minutes.

SHORTBREAD

1 cup butter or margarine
$\frac{3}{4}$ cup castor sugar or pure icing sugar
3 cups plain flour
1 teaspoon baking powder

1. Cream butter and sugar.
2. Add flour and baking powder, sifted.
3. Mix thoroughly.
4. Turn onto a slightly floured board.
5. Divide into 18 pieces.

(continued)

6. Flatten till about 1 cm thick and pinch frill round edges.
7. Glaze with egg, and decorate with small pieces peel or cherries.
8. Place on greased slide.
9. Bake in very moderate oven, 150°–180°C, for 20 to 30 minutes.

SNAP OR CRISP BISCUITS

$\frac{1}{2}$ cup butter
$\frac{1}{2}$ cup sugar
Vanilla to taste
1 egg (45 g) beaten
1 cup self-raising flour

1. Cream butter and sugar and vanilla.
2. Add egg, beat well.
3. Sift in flour all at once. Stir till well mixed.
4. Drop small sections from spoon onto greased tray.
5. Bake at 140°–160°C for 10 to 15 minutes, until golden brown.

Note. $\frac{1}{2}$ teaspoon of grated lemon or orange rind may be added for variety.

WHEATMEAL BISCUITS

$\frac{1}{2}$ cup butter or margarine
$\frac{1}{2}$ cup sugar
1 egg (60 g)
Vanilla to taste
2 cups self-raising flour
1 cup fine wheatmeal
Pinch salt

1. Grease an oven slide.
2. Cream butter and sugar.
3. Add egg and vanilla. Beat well.
4. Add flour and wheatmeal.
5. Roll on floured board.
6. Cut thinly.
7. Glaze with water or milk.
8. Bake at 150° – 180° for 10 to 15 minutes.

SCONE AND LOAF MIXTURES

SCONES

2 cups self-raising flour
$\frac{1}{4}$ teaspoon salt
2 tablespoons butter or
    margarine
1 cup milk

1. Have a hot oven in readiness.
2. Grease an oven slide.
3. Sift flour and salt together.
4. Rub butter in lightly with tips of fingers.
5. Pour nearly all the milk in at once, keeping a little for glazing.
6. Mix quickly into a soft dough.
7. Turn onto floured board; knead lightly and quickly.
8. Roll or press out to a round shape about 2 cm thick.
9. Cut into 6 triangular pieces using a floured knife, or use a plain round cutter.
10. Glaze with milk.
11. Cook quickly, 8 to 10 minutes, in a hot oven, 230°–260°C.
12. Cool.

Variations

1. Roll or press out the dough. Spread with grated cheese, sprinkle with salt and pepper. Roll up like a Swiss roll. Using a sharp knife cut into 1–2 cm pieces. Places onto well-greased slide, with the cut edge up. Bake as above.
2. Anchovy or ham paste may be used instead of cheese.

Note. Plain scone mixtures may be pressed out the size of saucepan or casserole and placed on top of stews or stewed fruits. Cook 20 to 30 minutes with lid on tightly.

CHEESE LOAF OR SCONES

2 cups self-raising flour
1 tablespoon butter
$\frac{1}{2}$ cup grated cheese
Pinch salt
2 tablespoons sugar
     (optional)
1 egg
$\frac{1}{2}$ cup milk

1. Sift flour.
2. Rub in butter and cheese.
3. Add salt and sugar.
4. Moisten with beaten egg and milk.
5. Shape into scones or place in greased loaf pan.
6. Bake loaf in a moderate oven, 200°–220°C, for 20 minutes; bake scones at 220°–260°C for 8 to 10 minutes.

PUFTALOONS (FRIED SCONES)

1 cup self-raising flour
Pinch salt
$\frac{1}{2}$ cup milk
Clarified fat

1. Sift flour and salt.
2. Add milk nearly all at once, and make into a soft dough.
3. Turn onto a floured board and knead slightly.
4. Press out about 1 cm thick.
5. Cut with a small round cutter.
6. Make a small quantity of clarified fat moderately hot in a small frying pan.
7. Put the puftaloons in and fry gently until golden brown underneath, then turn with a knife and cook till the other side is browned.
8. Drain on absorbent paper.
9. Serve hot with honey, golden syrup, or jam.

DATE OR SULTANA SCONES

$\frac{1}{3}$ cup sultanas or dates
2 cups self-raising flour
$\frac{1}{4}$ teaspoon salt
2 tablespoons butter
3 tablespoons sugar
1 egg
$\frac{2}{3}$ cup milk

1. Attend to oven.
2. Sprinkle a little flour on an oven slide or baking dish.
3. Wash, stem, and dry sultanas, or chop dates.
4. Sift flour and salt.
5. Rub in butter lightly with tips of fingers until quite free from lumps.
6. Add sugar and sultanas or dates.
7. Beat egg well, and add the milk to it.

(continued)

8. Pour into the dry ingredients, nearly all at once, enough to make a moist dough. Leave a little for glazing.
9. Turn onto a floured board and knead lightly.
10. Roll or press out about 1–2 cm thick.
11. Stamp into rounds with a small cutter.
12. Glaze with the remainder of the egg and milk glazing.
13. Place on prepared slide or baking dish.
14. Bake in a hot oven, 230°–260°C, for about 12 minutes.
15. When cooked, turn onto a cooler.

Variations

1. Add 1 tablespoon of finely grated orange rind instead of fruit.
2. Omit fruit from mixture and
   (a) Roll or press out the dough.
   Glaze with milk.
   Sprinkle with brown sugar and mixed fruit.
   Roll up like a Swiss roll.
   Using a sharp knife cut into 1–2 cm pieces.
   Place on a well-greased slide, with cut edge up.
   Bake as above.
   (b) Cream 2 tablespoons butter and 3 tablespoons brown sugar.
   Spread on dough, sprinkle with cinnamon, and roll out. Cut and bake as above.

GEM SCONES

2 tablespoons butter or margarine
3 tablespoons sugar
1 egg
4 tablespoons milk
$1\frac{1}{4}$ cups self-raising flour
$\frac{1}{4}$ teaspoon salt

1. Heat gem irons.
2. Beat butter and sugar to a cream.
3. Add egg and beat well.
4. Add milk.
5. Add sifted flour and salt, and mix lightly.
6. Place into heated, greased gem irons.
7. Bake in a hot oven, 230°–250°C, for 7 to 10 minutes.

PUMPKIN SCONES

2 tablespoons butter
2 tablespoons sugar
$\frac{1}{2}$ cup mashed pumpkin
1 egg
$\frac{1}{2}$ cup milk
$2\frac{1}{2}$ cups self-raising flour

1. Cream butter and sugar.
2. Add pumpkin.
3. Add well-beaten egg.
4. Add milk slowly.
5. Add sifted flour.
6. Knead lightly on floured board.
7. Roll out 2–3 cm thick.
8. Cut into rounds.
9. Put on floured tray.
10. Cook at 230°–260°C for 20 minutes.
11. Place on rack to cool.

CHERRY AND NUT RING

2 cups self-raising flour
Pinch salt
$\frac{1}{3}$ cup butter or margarine
$\frac{1}{3}$ cup sugar
1 egg
$\frac{2}{3}$ cup milk
$\frac{1}{2}$ cup chopped nuts
$\frac{1}{2}$ cup chopped cherries
$\frac{1}{2}$ teaspoon cinnamon

1. Sift flour and salt.
2. Rub in butter. Add sugar.
3. Beat egg and add to milk.
4. Add to other ingredients and mix into a soft dough.
5. Knead lightly and press or roll out to 1 cm thick.
6. Spread nuts, cherries, and cinnamon on dough.
7. Roll lengthwise, form into a ring on a greased flat pan or in a greased ring pan.
8. Cut slices 2 cm wide almost through with a sharp knife or kitchen scissors.
9. Bake at 200°–220°C for 20 to 25 minutes.

Variations

Instead of nuts, cherries, and cinnamon use:
  (a) 1 cup mixed fruit and 1 tablespoon sugar; or
  (b) 1 cup finely grated apple, $\frac{1}{2}$ tablespoon sugar, and 1 tablespoon grated lemon rind.

DATE LOAF

2 tablespoons butter or
    margarine
$\frac{1}{2}$ cup sugar
1 egg
$\frac{2}{3}$ cup milk
1 cup dates
$1\frac{1}{2}$ cups self-raising flour
Pinch salt

1. Beat butter and sugar to a cream.
2. Add well-beaten egg.
3. Add milk gradually.
4. Add chopped dates.
5. Stir in lightly the sifted flour and salt.
6. Half fill greased loaf pan.
7. Bake in a moderate oven, 180°–190°C, for 35 to 40 minutes.

Variations

Instead of dates use chopped ginger, cherries, and almonds or sultanas.

NUT LOAF

2 cups self-raising flour
Pinch salt
$\frac{1}{4}$ cup sugar
$\frac{1}{2}$ cup walnuts or mixed nuts
1 egg
1 cup milk

1. Sift flour, salt, and sugar.
2. Add chopped nuts.
3. Beat egg and add to it the milk.
4. Add to the dry ingredients, making into a soft dough.
5. Place into greased loaf pans.
6. Bake in a moderate oven, 180°–190°C, for 45 minutes to 1 hour.

Note. This quantity is sufficient for two small loaves.

COFFEE ROLLS

$\frac{1}{3}$ cup butter
$\frac{1}{2}$ cup sugar
1 egg (60 g)
1 cup milk
4 cups self-raising flour

1. Cream butter and sugar.
2. Add beaten egg; beat well.
3. Add milk.
4. Stir in sifted flour.
5. Mix well to a soft dough.
6. Roll on a floured board 1 cm thick.
7. Cut into rounds; fold over and glaze.
8. Bake in hot oven, 230°–260°C, for 10 minutes.

BREADS AND YEAST COOKERY

BROWN BREAD

40 g (2 tablespoons) compressed yeast
2 cups warm water
3 cups plain flour
1 tablespoon salt
3 cups fine wheatmeal
1 tablespoon sugar
1 tablespoon lard or butter

1. Crumble yeast into a small basin.
2. Add $\frac{2}{3}$ cup water, mix well, and set aside.
3. Sift flour and salt into a large basin.
4. Add wheatmeal and sugar. Mix well.
5. Rub in lard or butter.
6. Make a well in the centre of the flour mixture and pour in the yeast and water mixture.
7. Mix to a soft dough with the remaining water.
8. Turn out onto a floured board.
9. Knead well until the dough is smooth, satiny and not sticky. Dough is ready if it springs back when pressed lightly with a finger.
10. Form dough into a ball, cover with a clean cloth, and stand in a warm place for 10 minutes.
11. Knead dough lightly to break any large gas bubbles that may have formed.
12. Divide dough in half. Form each piece into a ball.
13. Place on a well-greased oven tray.
14. Cover with a cloth and a piece of plastic.
15. Stand in a warm place until dough has doubled in bulk. 30 to 40 minutes.
16. Bake in a hot oven, 230°–260°C, for 25 to 35 minutes.

Note. Dough may be moulded into loaves and baked in pans (see White Bread (1) p. 134).
For wholemeal bread omit white flour and use 6 cups fine wheatmeal.

"DRIBARM" BREAD

1.5 kg plain flour
2 tablespoons salt
2 tablespoons sugar
1 tablespoon "Dribarm"
    yeast
4 cups warm water
1 tablespoon melted butter

1. Sift flour and salt into a basin.
2. Mix sugar and yeast in 1½ cups of the water.
3. Make a well in the centre of the dry ingredients and pour in the yeast mixture and melted butter.
4. With a wooden spoon, mix enough of the flour with the liquid to form a thin batter.
5. Cover with a clean cloth and a piece of plastic, and let stand in a warm place for about 1 hour until the sponge rises.
6. Gradually add enough lukewarm water to make a soft dough.
7. Turn onto a floured board.
8. Knead until dough becomes smooth and satiny.
9. Place in a greased basin, turning dough over once.
10. Cover with a clean cloth and a piece of plastic.
11. Stand in a warm place until dough doubles in bulk.
12. Punch down and knead lightly to break any large gas bubbles.
13. Divide dough, shape as desired, and place in greased pans. Pans should be half full.
14. Cover with cloth and plastic and stand in a warm place until double in bulk.
15. Bake in a hot oven, 230°–260°C, until well risen and brown, about 25 to 30 minutes.

WHITE BREAD (1)

1 kg plain flour
20 g (1 tablespoon) compressed yeast
1 tablespoon sugar
2½ cups warm water
    (variable)
1 tablespoon salt

1. Sift flour.
2. Place in a warm basin and make a well in the centre.
3. Crumble yeast into the well, sprinkle in sugar and pour in about 2 tablespoons of the water. Mix into a batter.
4. Let it stand in a warm place till it rises well (10 to 15 minutes).

(continued)

5. Sprinkle the salt on the flour.
6. Mix to a soft dough using the remaining warm water.
7. Turn onto a floured board.
8. Knead well until the dough is smooth, satiny and not sticky. Dough is ready if it springs back when pressed lightly with a finger.
9. Place in a warmed, greased basin. Turn dough over so the surface is greased.
10. Cover with a cloth and a piece of plastic to prevent surface drying.
11. Stand in a warm place until the dough has doubled in bulk (35 to 40 minutes).
12. Lift dough onto floured board.
13. Knead lightly to break any large gas bubbles.
14. Divide dough into three pieces (one for each pan).
15. Roll each out to a rectangle as wide as the pans are long.
16. Roll up like a Swiss roll starting from the short side. Seal the edge but not the ends.
17. Place in well-greased pans, sealed edge down. Pans should be about half full.
18. Cover and let stand in a warm place until dough has risen above the tops of the pans (10 to 20 minutes).
19. Bake in a hot oven, 230°–260°C, for 25 to 30 minutes. If cooked, the loaf will sound hollow when tapped on top.
20. Turn onto cake cooler, leave until cool.

WHITE BREAD (2) (WITH MILK)

1¼ cups milk (or milk and water)
1 tablespoon sugar
500 g plain flour
1 tablespoon salt
1 tablespoon butter or lard
20 g (1 tablespoon) compressed yeast

1. Scald milk, add sugar. Cool to lukewarm.
2. Sift flour and salt into a warm basin.
3. Rub in butter or lard.
4. Crumble yeast into milk and sugar mixture and stir well.
5. Make a well in the centre of the flour and pour in milk mixture.
6. Mix to a soft dough.
7. Turn onto a floured board.

8. Knead until dough is smooth and satiny (about 10 minutes).
9. Cover with a clean cloth and a piece of plastic, and stand in a warm place for 10 minutes.
10. Shape and mould as desired.
11. Place on greased trays. Cover with a cloth and a piece of plastic.
12. Stand in a warm place until dough has doubled in bulk.
13. Bake on the trays in a hot oven, 230°–260°C, until well risen and golden, about 25 to 30 minutes. If cooked, bread will sound hollow when tapped on top.

STOLLEN

1 tablespoon compressed yeast
3 tablespoons lukewarm water
3 cups plain flour
2 eggs
60 ml evaporated milk
$\frac{1}{2}$ cup sugar
1 teaspoon vanilla
$\frac{1}{8}$ teaspoon lemon essence
$\frac{1}{2}$ teaspoon salt
Pinch cardamom
$\frac{1}{2}$ cup butter, melted
250 g (1$\frac{1}{2}$ cups) mixed dried fruit

1. Dissolve yeast in water.
2. Add 3 tablespoons of the flour and mix well.
3. Cover and stand in a warm place for 25 minutes or until the sponge rises and falls back.
4. Beat eggs with evaporated milk, sugar, vanilla, and lemon essence.
5. Sift remainder of the flour, salt and cardamom together into a basin.
6. Add milk mixture and sponge.
7. Mix well to make a soft dough.
8. Add melted butter and mix until butter is incorporated and dough smooth.
9. Turn onto a floured board.
10. Knead for 5 minutes.
11. Knead in mixed dried fruit, adding an extra tablespoon of flour if necessary.
12. Cover with a cloth and stand in a warm place for 10 minutes.
13. Divide dough into 2 pieces.
14. Roll each piece out to an oval shape on a lightly floured board.
15. Brush surface of each piece with a little melted butter.
16. Fold one rounded end over to within 2 cm of the opposite end.

(continued)

17. Place on greased oven trays.
18. Cover each tray with a piece of plastic and a cloth.
19. Stand in a warm place until almost double in size (approximately 30 minutes).
20 Bake in a moderate oven, 200°–220°C, for 25 minutes or until well risen and golden brown.
21. Remove from oven, brush with melted butter, and sprinkle with sugar flavoured with vanilla.

YEAST BUNS

$\frac{1}{3}$ cup skim milk powder
$\frac{1}{3}$ cup sugar
1 cup water
3 tablespoons butter
40 g (2 tablespoons) compressed yeast
500 g plain flour
2 teaspoons salt
$\frac{1}{2}$ cup sultanas

Glazing
1 teaspoon gelatine
1 tablespoon sugar
1 tablespoon hot water

1. Mix skim milk powder and sugar together in a saucepan. Add $\frac{2}{3}$ cup of the water. Mix until smooth.
2. Heat, stirring constantly, until boiling.
3. Add butter and remaining water. Cool to lukewarm, then add crumbled yeast.
4. Sift flour and salt together. Add sultanas.
5. Add milk mixture and mix well to make a soft dough (add more warm water if necessary).
6. Knead well for 10 minutes (dough should be satiny).
7. Place in a greased bowl, cover with plastic, and stand in a warm place for 10 minutes.
8. Divide dough into 16 even-sized pieces. Shape into buns.
9. Place on greased slides, and stand in a warm place until they double in bulk (20 to 30 minutes).
10. Bake in a moderately hot oven, 200°–230°C, for 15 to 20 minutes.
11. Glaze immediately with gelatine and sugar dissolved in the hot water.

SANDWICHES

TYPES

Lunch pack

Two slices of bread spread with butter and generous layer of filling between.

Toasted

Make as above, toast both sides and serve immediately. Crusts may be trimmed.

Open

One slice of bread with a firm crisp crust, spread with butter and covered with a variety of foods arranged attractively.

Club or doubledecker

Three or more slices of buttered bread or toast with a different filling for each layer.

Fancy sandwiches for afternoon tea or parties

Ribbon. Four slices of bread, two brown and two white. Butter bread, spread with smooth savoury filling. Arrange brown and white bread alternately. Press lightly, cut across into fingers and arrange on a plate to show the strips.
Pinwheels. Use unsliced sandwich loaf, remove crusts, slice thinly lengthwise, butter and spread with soft filling, roll as for a Swiss roll. Wrap in plastic wrap or greaseproof paper. Chill, then slice.
Rolled Sandwiches. Remove crusts from slices of fresh sandwich loaves. Spread with creamed butter, cover with filling or place a length of asparagus. Roll up, secure with cocktail sticks, and chill. Remove sticks before serving.

GENERAL RULES FOR MAKING

1. Prepare bread.
2. Soften butter.
3. Spread fillings generously.
4. Place second slice on top of filling, press lightly.
5. Trim edges if necessary.
6. Cut.
7. If for packed lunches wrap in plastic film, greaseproof or waxed paper.
8. If for serving at home arrange on plates, garnish with parsley sprigs, shredded lettuce or celery curls.

FILLINGS

Cheese

Sliced or grated, plain or with chopped nuts, chives, parsley, celery, apple, grated carrot, sliced cucumber, tomato or with chutney.

Cream cheese

Beat till smooth then add chopped onion, celery, capsicum, dates, raisins, ginger, nuts, pineapple, chopped ham or a combination of any of these.

Meats

Any cold cooked meats, sliced thinly or minced and mixed with sauce or chutney.

Fish

Flaked smoked fish mixed with a little white sauce and chopped parsley.
Tuna mixed with a little mayonnaise or cream, chopped gherkin or tomato.
Salmon, mixed with a little lemon juice.
Sardines, mixed with a little lemon juice.

Eggs

Scrambled. For variety add curry powder, chives, parsley or chopped bacon.
Hard cooked, mashed with butter or cream.

Peanut butter

With shredded cabbage, grated carrot, mashed banana or chopped raisins.

Sandwich spreads

Vegetable extracts

SAUCES AND GRAVY

APPLE SAUCE

2 apples
1 teaspoon lemon juice
1 tablespoon water
2 teaspoons butter
1 tablespoon sugar

1. Peel, core, and slice apples.
2. Put in a saucepan with lemon juice, water, butter, and sugar.
3. Simmer till tender.
4. Beat with a wooden spoon until smooth.
5. Serve with roast pork, roast duck, or goose.

BREAD SAUCE

1 cup milk
$\frac{1}{2}$ blade mace (optional)
1 shallot
4 tablespoons fresh white breadcrumbs
2 teaspoons butter
$\frac{1}{4}$ teaspoon salt

1. Put milk, mace, and shallot into a saucepan and bring to the boil.
2. Strain.
3. Return milk to the saucepan.
4. Add breadcrumbs, butter, and salt.
5. Beat well with a wooden spoon.
6. Return to stove and stir while reheating.
7. Serve with roast fowl.

BROWN GRAVY

$1\frac{1}{2}$ tablespoons plain flour
Pinch pepper
$\frac{1}{2}$ teaspoon salt
1 cup water or stock

1. Strain most of the fat out of the baking dish or frying pan after cooking meat.
2. Add flour, pepper, and salt to the dish or pan.
3. Brown over the heat, stirring with the back of a spoon.
4. When brown, add water or stock—all at once if cold; gradually if boiling or hot water is used.
5. Stir till boiling; if not sufficiently brown add a few drops of caramel.
6. Strain (if necessary) and serve.

Scones (p. 128), Date Loaf (p. 132), Pumpkin Scones (p. 131).

PLAIN BROWN SAUCE

1 tablespoon dripping
1 onion
1 tablespoon plain flour
$\frac{1}{2}$ teaspoon salt
Pinch pepper
1 cup water or stock
1 tablespoon Worcestershire
    sauce
1 teaspoon vinegar

1. Place dripping in a small saucepan and heat.
2. Peel onion and cut into dice.
3. Fry onion until well browned but not burnt.
4. Drain the fat off.
5. Add flour, pepper, and salt to the onion, and stir till it browns.
6. Add water or stock, all at once, and stir till it boils.
7. Add sauce and vinegar.
8. Simmer about 10 minutes.
9. Strain and serve hot as an accompaniment to cutlets, rissoles, sausage rolls, etc.

CARAMEL SAUCE (1)

1 cup brown sugar
2 tablespoons water
1 tablespoon butter
2 tablespoons condensed
    milk

1. Place sugar, water, and butter in saucepan.
2. Stir over heat till sugar dissolves; boil 1 minute.
3. Remove from heat and stir in condensed milk.

CARAMEL SAUCE (2)

1 tablespoon butter
$\frac{1}{3}$ cup brown sugar
2 tablespoons condensed
    milk
1 tablespoon golden syrup
4 tablespoons hot water

1. Place butter, sugar, condensed milk, and syrup in a saucepan.
2. Stir over medium heat till a rich caramel colour and it leaves the sides of the saucepan (8 to 10 minutes).
3. Remove from heat, add water a little at a time, return to heat and stir until mixture boils and becomes smooth (about 1 minute). Sauce thickens as it cools.

Chutneys, pickles and jams (pp. 146–51).

CUSTARD SAUCE

1 tablespoon custard powder
2 teaspoons sugar
1 cup milk

1. Blend custard powder and sugar with a little milk.
2. Boil remainder of milk.
3. Add boiling milk to blended mixture, stirring well.
4. Return to saucepan and stir over heat till boiling.
5. Boil gently 2 minutes.

HORSE-RADISH SAUCE

1 root horse-radish or 1 tablespoon powdered horse-radish
3 tablespoons cream
2 tablespoons milk
1 teaspoon prepared mustard
2 teaspoons sugar
$\frac{1}{4}$ teaspoon salt
Pinch white pepper
1 tablespoon vinegar

1. Scrape horse-radish finely and mix with cream, milk, mustard, sugar, salt, and pepper.
2. Work vinegar in a drop at a time.

JAM, TREACLE, OR GOLDEN SYRUP SAUCE

1 tablespoon arrowroot
1 cup water
2 teaspoons sugar
3 tablespoons jam, treacle, or syrup
A few drops colouring (optional)
1 teaspoon lemon juice

1. Blend arrowroot with a little of the water.
2. Put remainder of water on to boil with the sugar and jam, syrup, or treacle.
3. Just before boiling, remove from heat, add blended arrowroot, and mix thoroughly.
4. Return to heat, stir until boiling, and simmer gently for 3 minutes.
5. Remove from heat and add colouring and lemon juice.

LEMON SAUCE

1 tablespoon arrowroot or 1½ tablespoons cornflour
1 cup water
½ teaspoon grated lemon rind
1 tablespoon sugar
2 tablespoons lemon juice

1. Blend arrowroot or cornflour with a little cold water.
2. Boil remaining water and lemon rind.
3. Add blended arrowroot, mix thoroughly, and stir until it boils and thickens. Cook 3 minutes.
4. Remove from heat and add sugar and lemon juice.

MINT SAUCE

2 tablespoons chopped green mint
2 tablespoons white sugar
1 tablespoon boiling water
2 tablespoons vinegar

1. Wash and dry mint, remove stalks.
2. Chop very finely.
3. Boil sugar and water for 1 minute.
4. Add mint and vinegar.
5. Pour into container to cool.
6. Stir well before serving.
7. Serve in a small glass jug as an accompaniment to roast lamb.

ECONOMICAL SAVOURY SAUCE (NO FAT)

1½ tablespoons plain flour
1 cup milk
¼ teaspoon salt

1. Blend flour with a little of the milk.
2. Put remainder of milk and salt on to boil in a saucepan.
3. When nearly boiling, remove from heat and add the blended flour, stirring well with a wooden spoon.
4. Return to stove and stir over heat for 3 minutes.

BASIC WHITE OR MELTED BUTTER SAUCE

Type	Butter or Margarine	Flour (plain)	Milk	Use
1. Pouring or Thin	1 tablespoon	1 tablespoon	1 cup	Cream Soups
2. Medium	1½ tablespoons	1½ tablespoons	1 cup	Vegetables Boiled meats Fish. Puddings
3. Thick or Masking	2 tablespoons	2 tablespoons	1 cup	Masking Sauce Souffles Scalloped foods Savoury fillings
4. Panada	3 tablespoons	3 tablespoons	1 cup	Binding Croquettes

Salt and pepper to taste.

1. Melt butter in saucepan—do not boil.
2. Remove from heat, add flour—and salt and pepper to taste. Stir with wooden spoon until smooth.
3. Stir over low heat for 1 minute—it must not be allowed to brown.
4. Add milk.
5. Stir over heat until it boils and thickens.

PARSLEY SAUCE

To basic white sauce recipe add 2 tablespoons finely chopped parsley.

ONION SAUCE

To basic white sauce recipe add ½ cup cooked chopped onion.

CAPER SAUCE

To basic white sauce recipe add 2 tablespoons capers.

CHEESE SAUCE

To basic white sauce recipe add ½ cup grated cheese.

CURRY SAUCE

Use basic white sauce recipe but add 2 teaspoons curry powder to flour.

MUSTARD SAUCE

Use basic white sauce recipe but add 2 teaspoons mustard to flour.

ANCHOVY SAUCE

To basic white sauce recipe add 2 teaspoons concentrated anchovy sauce or paste and ½ teaspoon lemon juice.

SWEET SAUCE

Use basic white sauce recipe but instead of salt and pepper add 1 tablespoon of sugar or 2 tablespoons of golden syrup.

SWEET WHITE SAUCE

1½ tablespoons maize cornflour
1 cup milk
1 tablespoon sugar
Vanilla essence

1. Blend cornflour with a little milk.
2. Put remainder of milk and sugar on to boil in a saucepan.
3. When nearly boiling remove from the heat, add the blended cornflour stirring it in with a wooden spoon.
4. Stir over heat for 3 minutes, add vanilla.
5. Serve as an accompaniment to puddings.

CHUTNEY, PICKLES, AND BOTTLED SAUCE

APPLE CHUTNEY

5 large cooking apples
500 g onions
1½ cups sultanas or raisins
500 g brown sugar
3 cups vinegar
½ cup water
2 teaspoons dry mustard
2 teaspoons salt
¼ teaspoon cayenne pepper
¼ teaspoon black pepper

1. Peel apples and onions. Cut into small pieces.
2. Place in saucepan with all other ingredients.
3. Stir over heat till boiling.
4. Cook slowly—at least 2 hours.
5. Bottle in warm jars and seal when cool.

CHOKO CHUTNEY

1 kg chokoes
½ tablespoon salt
2 cups vinegar
30 g chillies
4 cloves garlic
30 g whole ginger
500 g brown sugar
⅔ cup sultanas

1. Peel chokoes and cut into long strips. Sprinkle with salt and let stand overnight.
2. Boil vinegar, add chokoes, and simmer till soft.
3. Cut chillies, garlic, and ginger into small pieces.
4. Add with sugar and sultanas to the chokoes and vinegar.
5. Simmer gently until clear and rich brown in colour—about 2 hours.
6. Bottle in warm jars and seal when cool.

DATE CHUTNEY

500 g stoned dates
1 tablespoon salt
1 tablespoon dry mustard
1 tablespoon ground ginger
1 teaspoon cinnamon
1 cup boiling water
1 cup vinegar

1. Chop dates finely.
2. Boil all ingredients together for 5 minutes.
3. Bottle in warm jars and seal when cool.

MUSTARD PICKLE

1 kg cauliflower or chokoes or green tomatoes, or a mixture of all three
500 g onions
250 g beans
1 tablespoon salt
Enough vinegar to cover vegetables (3–4 cups)
$\frac{1}{2}$ teaspoon mixed spice
1 cup golden syrup
12 cloves
12 peppercorns
1 tablespoon dry mustard
1 tablespoon curry powder
1 tablespoon plain flour

1. Wash and prepare vegetables. Cut into convenient-size pieces.
2. Place in basin, sprinkle with salt, and let stand overnight.
3. Put vinegar, spice, and syrup on to boil, adding cloves and peppercorns tied in a muslin bag.
4. Drain vegetables. Add to boiling vinegar.
5. Boil 20 minutes or till crisp. Remove bag.
6. Blend mustard, curry powder, and flour with a little vinegar.
7. Add to saucepan and simmer 10 minutes.
8. Bottle in warm jars and seal when cool.

PLUM SAUCE

3 kg plums
1·5 kg white sugar
$\frac{1}{2}$ teaspoon pepper
$\frac{1}{4}$ teaspoon cayenne pepper
5 cups vinegar
1 tablespoon salt
1 onion
1 tablespoon ground ginger

1. Wash plums.
2. Place all ingredients in pan; stir till sugar dissolves.
3. Boil until stones separate from fruit.
4. Strain through a coarse strainer and bottle in warm jars.
5. Cork or seal when sauce is cold.

TOMATO SAUCE

3 kg ripe tomatoes
250 g apples
250 g onions
2 cloves garlic
1 cup sugar
2 tablespoons salt
1 chilli
$\frac{1}{2}$ tablespoon cloves
$\frac{1}{2}$ tablespoon peppercorns
1 teaspoon curry powder
$2\frac{1}{2}$ cups vinegar

1. Wash tomatoes and cut up roughly.
2. Peel and slice apples and onions.
3. Cut garlic up finely.
4. Place in saucepan; add all other ingredients.
5. Boil gently 2 hours.
6. Strain through a coarse strainer.
7. Bottle in warm jars and seal when cool.

TOMATO RELISH

1.5 kg tomatoes
500 g onions
2 cups sugar
$2\frac{1}{2}$ cups vinegar
1 tablespoon flour
1 tablespoon curry powder
Pinch cayenne
1 tablespoon dry mustard
1 tablespoon salt

1. Cut up tomatoes and pour off $\frac{3}{4}$ cup of juice.
2. Cut up onions finely.
3. Put in a saucepan with tomatoes, sugar, and vinegar.
4. Boil slowly until it thickens.
5. Blend flour, curry powder, cayenne, mustard, and salt with tomato juice.
6. Add to saucepan and stir until boiling.
7. Cook gently for 3 minutes.
8. Bottle in warm jars and seal when cool.

JAMS AND JELLIES

To ensure success the fruit should be firm, sound, and slightly under-ripe. Early fruits are best for jam-making.

As a general rule, 1½ cups sugar is used to each 500 g of fruit, or 1 cup sugar to each cup of pulp when making jam, and 1 cup sugar to 1 cup juice for jelly.

To test if cooked. Place a small quantity on a saucer; cool. If cooked it will jell and wrinkle when moved.

APPLE JELLY

Slightly under-ripe apples
Sugar (1 cup for each cup of juice)

1. Wash the apples, slice, and just cover with water.
2. Boil gently until soft—30 to 40 minutes.
3. Strain through a jelly flannel or clean linen cloth fastened securely above a basin.
4. Allow to drip through slowly. DO NOT squeeze.
5. Measure out one cup of sugar to each cup of juice.
6. Add sugar to the juice in saucepan.
7. Stir over heat until sugar dissolves.
8. Boil quickly until it jells when tested.
9. Remove any scum as it rises.
10. Pour into warm jars, seal, and label.

Note. Crabapples may be used with this recipe. Remove stalks and wash apples, but do not cut.

DRIED APRICOT JAM

2 cups dried apricots
2 litres water
1.5 kg sugar

1. Wash apricots.
2. Cover with water and allow to soak over-night or until soft.
3. Bring to the boil; cook gently until tender.
4. Add heated sugar.

(continued)

5. Stir carefully until the sugar is dissolved.
6. Cook quickly until the mixture jells when tested.
7. Pour into heated jars.
8. Seal and label.

BLACKBERRY JAM

500 g blackberries
1½ cups sugar

1. Remove stalks from berries and place in saucepan.
2. Cover with sugar and allow to stand about 1 hours.
3. Place over heat, stir occasionally until sugar is dissolved.
4. Boil till the jam will jell when tested.
5. Bottle in warm jars and seal.

Note. Strawberries or raspberries may be used instead of blackberries.

CARROT AND LEMON JAM

4 medium carrots
3 lemons
2 litres water
2 kg sugar

1. Grate carrots and cut lemons finely.
2. Cover with water and let stand overnight.
3. Bring to the boil and boil $1\frac{1}{4}$ hours.
4. Add sugar, stir till dissolved.
5. Boil until the jam will jell when tested, about $\frac{3}{4}$ to 1 hour.
6. Bottle in warm jars and seal.

GRAPEFRUIT JAM

500 g grapefruit
5 cups water
1 kg sugar

1. Cut fruit thinly and remove pips; add water and allow to stand overnight.
2. Bring to the boil and simmer gently until skins are tender.
3. Add warmed sugar; stir till boiling.
4. Boil quickly until it jells when tested.
5. Allow to stand until fruit begins to sink.
6. Bottle in warm jars and seal.

MARMALADE

2 medium oranges
1 lemon
2 litres water
1 kg sugar

1. Wash and slice fruit thinly; remove the seeds.
2. Place in a container, cover with water, and let stand overnight.
3. Boil fruit and water until rind is soft—about 1 hour.
4. Add sugar all at once; stir until dissolved.
5. Boil until it will jell when tested.
6. Bottle in warm jars and seal.

PLUM JAM

2 kg plums
1.5 kg sugar

1. Wash plums; remove stones if possible.
2. Cook with a little of the sugar until fruit is tender.
3. Add the remaining sugar (heated).
4. When sugar is dissolved, cook rapidly until the jam will jell when tested.
5. Pour into heated jars and seal.

Note. Peaches, apricots, or nectarines may be used instead of plums.

TOMATO JAM

2 kg tomatoes
3 lemons
3 tablespoons preserved ginger
1.75 kg sugar

1. Wash tomatoes. Cut into pieces.
2. Peel lemons finely and cut the peel into thin shreds.
3. Grate or chop the ginger.
4. Squeeze juice from lemons.
5. Place tomatoes, ginger, sugar, lemon peel, and lemon juice in saucepan.
6. Stir over heat until boiling.
7. Boil until the jam will jell when tested.
8. Pour into heated jars and seal.

SWEETS AND CONFECTIONERY

APPLES ON STICKS

6 red apples
6 wooden skewers
1 cup cold water
500 g sugar
2 tablespoons vinegar

1. Grease an oven slide.
2. Wash and dry apples. Place a skewer through the core of each.
3. Boil water, sugar, and vinegar to 154°C measured on sweets thermometer, or until syrup turns golden brown.
4. Stand saucepan in a basin of hot water.
5. Dip apples in toffee and coat well.
6. Place on greased slide to set.

COCONUT ICE

$\frac{1}{2}$ cup milk
2 cups sugar
Pinch cream of tartar
$\frac{1}{2}$ cup desiccated coconut

1. Put milk, sugar, and cream of tartar into saucepan.
2. Stir over low heat until sugar dissolves and the mixture boils.
3. Remove spoon. Boil 5 minutes.
4. Cool slightly, then beat well.
5. When beginning to thicken, add coconut and continue beating till mixture is quite thick.
6. Pour into a greased cake pan.
7. When cold, cut into squares.

UNCOOKED COCONUT ICE

60 g cream cheese
3 cups pure icing sugar
2 teaspoons milk
$\frac{1}{2}$ teaspoon vanilla
$\frac{1}{2}$ cup desiccated coconut
Pink food colouring

1. Beat cream cheese.
2. Add icing sugar gradually, and beat well.
3. Stir in milk, vanilla, and coconut.
4. Stir or knead till smooth.
5. Colour half pink.
6. Press white half into a well-greased cake pan. Cover with pink half.
7. Chill and cut into pieces.

UNCOOKED FONDANT

2 teaspoons glucose
1 egg white
500 g pure icing sugar
$\frac{1}{4}$ teaspoon lemon juice
3 drops vanilla
Food colouring

1. Melt glucose in cup standing in boiling water.
2. Drop slightly beaten egg white into centre of icing sugar. Cover with a little icing sugar.
3. Add glucose and stir well with a wooden spoon.
4. When sugar is almost absorbed, turn onto a board dusted with icing sugar and knead until smooth.
5. Add flavourings and colouring.

GINGER OR CHERRY CREAMS

$\frac{1}{2}$ cup milk
2 cups sugar
Pinch cream of tartar
$\frac{3}{4}$ cup preserved ginger or cherries
2 teaspoons butter

1. Place milk and sugar in saucepan.
2. Stir over low heat until sugar dissolves and the mixture boils.
3. Add cream of tartar and cherries or ginger.
4. Stir and bring to boiling point. Add butter.
5. Remove spoon. Boil 6 minutes.
6. Cool slightly, then stir till mixture thickens.
7. Press into pans lined with waxed or grease-proof paper.
8. When cold, cut into pieces.

FRENCH JELLIES

4 tablespoons powdered
    gelatine
2 cups cold water
4 cups sugar
Pinch cream of tartar
Icing sugar

1. Soak gelatine in half the water.
2. Place rest of water, sugar, and cream of tartar in saucepan.
3. Bring to boil, stirring gently until sugar is dissolved.
4. Add gelatine and simmer gently 20 minutes.
5. Pour into wetted plates or pans.
6. When cold, cut into squares and toss in icing sugar.

MARSHMALLOWS

3 tablespoons gelatine
1 cup cold water
4 cups sugar
$1\frac{1}{2}$ cups hot water
Vanilla or lemon essence to
    taste
Icing sugar
Cornflour

1. Soak gelatine in cold water.
2. Bring sugar and hot water to boiling point.
3. Add soaked gelatine.
4. Boil gently 20 minutes.
5. Pour into a large mixing bowl. Cool and add essence.
6. Beat until thick.
7. Pour into wetted 28 × 18 cm slab cake pan.
8. When cold, cut into squares and toss in a mixture of icing sugar and cornflour.

PLAIN TOFFEE

2 cups sugar
$\frac{3}{4}$ cup cold water
1 tablespoon vinegar

1. Place all ingredients in saucepan.
2. Stir over heat until sugar is dissolved.
3. Bring to boil—do not stir.
4. Cook until syrup is golden brown.
5. Remove from heat, allow bubbles to settle.
6. Pour into small paper containers or into a flat greased pan and mark into squares.

DISHES SUITABLE FOR CONVALESCENTS, THE AGED, AND CHILDREN

APPLE DELIGHT

1 apple
1 tablespoon sugar
1 slice sponge cake
1 egg (60 g)

1. Wash and dry apple.
2. Remove the core, using an apple corer or pointed knife.
3. Place on an ovenproof dish with a little water, and bake till soft.
4. Scrape out the pulp with a spoon.
5. Add sugar to the pulp.
6. Crumble the cake into crumbs.
7. Add to the apple pulp.
8. Beat the egg and stir it in.
9. Put into a saucepan and stir briskly over heat till hot—it must not boil.
10. Arrange on a dish, and serve hot or cold with stirred custard (see p. 70).

Note. Apples may be stewed instead of baked.

BAKED APPLE

1 apple
1 teaspoon sugar
1 clove
A little butter
Icing sugar

1. Wash and dry apple.
2. Remove the core a little more than half way through from the flower.
3. Fill up this hole with sugar, clove, and butter.
4. Slit the skin around the centre to prevent the apple from bursting.
5. Place it in a small pie-dish with just a little water in the bottom to prevent it from sticking.
6. Bake in moderate oven, 180°–200°C, for 30 minutes or till tender.
7. Serve on a small plate with remaining syrup. Sprinkle with icing sugar.

ARROWROOT OR CORNFLOUR GRUEL

1 tablespoon arrowroot or
  maize cornflour
1¼ cups milk
Pinch of salt
1 teaspoon of sugar
Nutmeg (if allowed)

1. Blend arrowroot or cornflour with a little of the milk.
2. Put remainder of milk on to boil with salt and sugar.
3. When nearly boiling, remove from heat.
4. Add the blended arrowroot or cornflour; stir well.
5. Return to heat, bring to the boil, and simmer for 3 minutes.
6. Stir well.
7. Serve in a small bowl or cup.
8. Grate nutmeg on top (if allowed).
9. Serve sippets of toast separately on a small plate.

BARLEY WATER

2 tablespoons pearl barley
2½ cups boiling water
A small piece lemon rind

1. Wash barley.
2. Put into the saucepan of boiling water.
3. Add lemon rind.
4. Boil without lid until reduced to half quantity.
5. Strain.
6. Sweeten to taste and add little lemon juice.

QUICKLY MADE BEEF TEA

250 g gravy beef or lean steak
¼ teaspoon salt
2½ cups cold water
A few drops lemon juice

1. Remove all fat from meat.
2. Shred or mince very finely.
3. Put into a basin with salt, water, and lemon juice.
4. Cover and allow to stand for 1 hour.
5. Turn it all into a double saucepan and stir till it just changes colour and becomes hot.
6. Pour into a small bowl, keeping the meat back with a spoon.
7. Serve with sippets of toast.

RICH BEEF TEA

As for Quickly Made Beef Tea

1. Remove all fat from meat; gash well.
2. Put into basin with salt, water, and lemon juice. Cover and allow to stand for 1 hour.
3. Put into a double saucepan, or into a casserole or jug standing in another saucepan, and cook at a very low temperature for $1\frac{1}{2}$ to 2 hours.
4. Press meat well during cooking with back of spoon, to extract goodness.
5. Serve hot with sippets of toast.

Note. 1 teaspoon of soaked sago may be added during the cooking if desired.

BEEF TEA CUSTARD

1 egg yolk
$\frac{1}{2}$ cup beef tea (see above)
Salt and pepper added carefully, if allowed

1. Stir yolk of egg.
2. Add beef tea, and season with salt and pepper.
3. Pour into a buttered cup or mould.
4. Steam very gently until set, about 5 to 10 minutes.
5. Turn on to hot plate and serve.

BRAIN CAKES

2 sets brains
A small piece of onion
1 tablespoon butter
1 tablespoon plain flour
$\frac{2}{3}$ cup milk
$\frac{1}{4}$ teaspoon salt
Pinch cayenne pepper
A little grated nutmeg
2 tablespoons flour seasoned with salt and pepper
Egg glazing
Breadcrumbs

1. Wash brains and remove skin.
2. Put in a saucepan with onion and a little salt.
3. Cover with cold water.
4. Bring slowly to simmering point and cook slowly for 6 minutes.
5. Drain off the water and allow the brains to cool.
6. Cut brains into 1 cm pieces.
7. Melt butter in a small saucepan.
8. Add flour, and cook 1 or 2 minutes without browning.
9. Add the milk all at once; stir till it boils and thickens.

(continued)

10. Stir in the salt, cayenne, grated nutmeg, and chopped brains.
11. Turn out on a plate to cool.
12. When cold form the brain mixture into small round shapes in seasoned flour.
13. Dip in egg glazing and then in breadcrumbs making them firm with a knife.
14. Heat fat. Fry brain cakes till golden brown.
15. Drain on absorbent paper.
16. Serve on a hot plate, garnished with small sprigs of parsley.

FRICASSEED BRAINS

1 set brains
1 tablespoon butter
1 tablespoon flour
$\frac{1}{4}$ teaspoon salt
$\frac{2}{3}$ cup milk
$\frac{1}{4}$ teaspoon chopped parsley

1. Wash brains and remove skin.
2. Cover with cold water, bring to simmering point, and simmer for 6 minutes.
3. Melt butter in a small saucepan; remove from heat; add flour and salt.
4. Stir till all lumps disappear; return to stove and cook 1 minute, stirring all the time, being careful not to let burn.
5. Add milk all at once; stir till it thickens.
6. Cut the brains into 1 cm squares without breaking.
7. Add to the sauce; reheat.
8. Add chopped parsley.
9. Serve on a hot plate, and garnish with sippets of dry toast.

SCALLOPED BRAINS

1 set brains
Small piece onion
Masking sauce, $\frac{1}{2}$ quantity (see p. 144)
Squeeze lemon juice
Salt
Cayenne
2 tablespoons dried bread-crumbs
Butter

1. Wash brains and remove skin.
2. Place in saucepan with onion.
3. Cover with cold water and bring to simmering point.
4. Cook gently for 6 minutes, then strain.
5. Cut brains into small dice, and add to white sauce.
6. Add lemon juice and a little salt and cayenne.

(continued)

7. Grease a scallop mould, and sprinkle thickly with breadcrumbs.
8. Fill mould with brain mixture.
9. Cover with crumbs; put small piece of butter on top.
10. Place in a moderate oven till crumbs are lightly browned, about 10 minutes, or brown under a griller.
11. Serve with small sprigs of parsley and thin slices of bread and butter.

BREAD AND MILK

$1\frac{1}{4}$ cups milk
1 thick slice of bread
1 teaspoon sugar (optional)

1. Remove crusts and cut bread into 1 cm cubes.
2. Heat milk in a saucepan, add sugar, and pour over bread.
3. Serve hot.

LIGHT BREAD PUDDING

2 tablespoons fresh bread-crumbs
$\frac{2}{3}$ cup milk
1 tablespoon sugar
1 egg

1. Grease a small pie-dish.
2. Put breadcrumbs into a basin.
3. Heat milk and pour onto breadcrumbs.
4. Add sugar.
5. Separate white from yolk of egg.
6. Stir yolk into milk and breadcrumbs.
7. Beat white up stiffly, and stir very lightly into mixture.
8. Pour into greased pie-dish.
9. Stand pie-dish in a baking-dish containing cold water.
10. Bake in a slow oven, $150°-160°$C, for 10 to 15 minutes or until set.
11. Serve hot or cold.

CHICKEN BROTH

1 dressed chicken or fowl, or
    750 g chicken pieces
5 cups water
Salt and pepper to taste

1. Cut chicken into pieces, wipe with damp cloth, and put into a saucepan with water, add salt and pepper.
2. Simmer very gently for 3 to 4 hours.
3. Strain and remove the fat.
4. If liked, when reheating, a little rice may be added to broth.

Note. A young rabbit makes an excellent substitute for chicken.

STEWED CHOPS AND RICE

2 neck chops
$\frac{1}{2}$ teaspoon salt
$1\frac{1}{4}$ cups water
2 tablespoons rice
1 small onion

1. Wipe chops and remove skin.
2. Put into a saucepan with salt and chopped onion.
3. Cover with water.
4. Bring to boil.
5. Simmer gently for $\frac{1}{2}$ hour.
6. Sprinkle in the well-washed rice.
7. Simmer gently 1 hour longer, being careful that the rice does not stick or burn.
8. When cooked, lift chops onto a hot plate and pour the rice and gravy round them.

STEAMED CUSTARD

1 egg
1 teaspoon sugar
$\frac{1}{2}$ cup milk
2 drops vanilla essence
    (optional)
Nutmeg (optional)

1. Put a shallow saucepan containing about 5 cm of water on the stove to heat.
2. Grease a small basin with butter.
3. Beat egg and sugar well together.
4. Add milk and vanilla.
5. Pour into the basin; place greased paper on top.
6. Stand in the saucepan and simmer water gently 5 to 10 minutes, or until custard is set.
7. When cooked, turn out on small dish and grate nutmeg on top.

EGG FLIP

1 fresh egg
1 teaspoon sugar
Flavouring
$\frac{2}{3}$ cup warmed milk

1. Separate white from yolk of egg.
2. Mix yolk and sugar thoroughly.
3. Beat white until quite stiff.
4. Add yolk and sugar, then flavouring and milk.
5. Mix well.
6. Pour into a tumbler and serve.

GRUEL

2 tablespoons fine oatmeal
$1\frac{1}{4}$ cups milk
Pinch salt
1 teaspoon sugar

1. Blend oatmeal with 2 tablespoons of the milk.
2. Put remainder of milk on to boil with salt.
3. Pour slowly onto the oatmeal, stirring all the time.
4. Allow to stand for 1 minute to let the oatmeal settle.
5. Strain the milk back into the saucepan.
6. Stir till boiling, and allow to simmer gently for 10 minutes.
7. Add sugar and butter and nutmeg.
8. Pour into a cup within 1 cm of the top and serve.

JUNKET

$\frac{1}{2}$ junket tablet
$1\frac{1}{4}$ cups fresh milk
1 teaspoon sugar
5 drops vanilla essence (if allowed)
Nutmeg (if allowed)

1. Dissolve the tablet in 1 teaspoon water.
2. Warm milk to blood heat by placing it in a cup with sugar and vanilla, and standing cup in a basin of boiling water for 5 minutes.
3. Stir in the dissolved tablet.
4. Pour into a glass dish, grate nutmeg on top, and stand in a warm place to set.
5. Allow to cool.

LEMON DRINK

1 small lemon
2 lumps loaf sugar
1 cup boiling water

1. Wash the lemon, peel very thinly, rub loaf sugar over lemon to extract the oil; squeeze the juice.
2. Place a few thin strips of rind of the lemon, the juice and the sugar in a jug.
3. Pour the boiling water on and cover.
4. Allow to cool.
5. Strain, if required, through clean muslin or strainer.

MILK JELLY

1½ teaspoons gelatine
2 tablespoons hot water
1 cup milk
3 teaspoon sugar
3 drops vanilla or other suitable flavouring

1. Dissolve gelatine in hot water.
2. Warm milk; add sugar and flavouring.
3. Stir in dissolved gelatine.
4. Pour into moulds or suitable dish.
5. Chill until set, and turn out.

SAVOURY OMELET

2 eggs
¼ teaspoon parsley
¼ teaspoon each of thyme and marjoram, or any suitable savoury flavourings
Pinch salt
Pinch pepper
1 tablespoon butter

1. Separate whites from yolks of eggs.
2. Beat yolks; add parsley, thyme, marjoram, salt, and pepper.
3. Beat whites up very stiffly.
4. Mix very lightly with the seasoned yolks.
5. Heat omelet pan slowly.
6. Melt butter in pan; pour in mixture; allow to set over a gentle heat.
7. Brown very slightly on top either by putting under hot griller or turning very carefully with a large knife.
8. Serve on a very hot dish at once.

Note. Fresh eggs must always be used for omelets.

SWEET OMELET

3 eggs
1 teaspoon water
1 tablespoon sugar
Jam
Butter

1. Take yolks of 2 eggs and whites of 3 eggs.
2. Boil water and sugar, cool, and add to the yolks.
3. Beat whites stiffly.
4. Have ready a hot plate and some heated jam.
5. Heat omelet pan slowly.
6. Add the yolks to the whites and mix lightly.
7. Melt butter in pan and pour in the mixture.
8. Cook gently and shake occasionally till set.
9. When coloured slightly underneath, brown the top by placing in the oven or under the griller.
10. Lift onto a hot plate.
11. Spread heated jam on one half.
12. Fold the other half over.
13. Serve at once.

In addition to dishes included in this section, the following recipes in other sections of this book could also be suitable:

Broth
Tomato cream soup
Fish cream
Grilled fish
Steamed fish
Scalloped oysters
Grilled chops, steak or cutlets
Fricasseed lamb, chicken or rabbit
Fricasseed tripe
Angel's food

Apple snow
Blancmange
College pudding
Baked custards
Stirred custard
Fruit flummery
Lemon sago
Stewed fruit
Sweet poached eggs
Sponge sandwich

Poached, steamed or scrambled eggs

MISCELLANEOUS

BREADCRUMBS

1. To make white breadcrumbs, rub the crumb part of stale bread through a sieve or colander, or on a grater.
2. To make brown breadcrumbs, place crusts of bread and very stale pieces in a very slow oven, and allow them to thoroughly dry. Crush on a board with a rolling pin till very fine. Store in glass jars or bottles.

CARAMEL

2 level tablespoons sugar
$\frac{2}{3}$ cup water

1. Place the sugar with 1 teaspoon of the water in a small saucepan (an old steel or iron one is best).
2. Cook till it becomes dark brown all over.
3. Add remainder of the water; allow to simmer very gently till the consistency of treacle (about 15 minutes).
4. Allow to cool, and pour into a wide-necked glass jar or bottle.

CLARIFIED FAT

250 g mixed fat or suet
1 cup water

1. Remove any small pieces of meat from the fat.
2. Cut fat into small pieces, about 2 cm square.
3. Place in a large saucepan.
4. Add the water, and cook slowly for $\frac{1}{2}$ hour with lid on.

(continued)

5. Remove the lid and stir frequently till all the water has evaporated.
6. Continue cooking and stirring till the fat is melted and appears like a clear oil.
7. Strain, pressing the pieces well to extract all fat.
8. Allow to cool—it should then be very hard and white.

FORCEMEAT

4 tablespoons white bread-crumbs
2 tablespoons butter or minced suet
1 tablespoon chopped parsley
$\frac{1}{4}$ teaspoon mixed chopped thyme and marjoram
A little grated lemon rind and nutmeg
$\frac{1}{4}$ teaspoon salt
Pinch pepper
1 well-beaten egg

1. Mix all ingredients, except egg, well together.
2. Add beaten egg and stir well.

Note. This may be used for fowls, turkeys, rabbit, and veal. For a turkey, mix $\frac{1}{2}$ cup sausage meat with the forcemeat.

GREEN BUTTER (PARSLEY BUTTER)
(for steak or grilled cutlets)

2 teaspoons butter
2 teaspoons chopped parsley
A few drops lemon juice
$\frac{1}{4}$ teaspoon salt
A little cayenne (optional)

Mix all ingredients together and spread over the meat.

PINK SUGAR
Place 1 drop of cochineal on 1 tablespoon of crystallized sugar, and mix well with the back of a spoon till a uniform colour. Pink sugar is sprinkled over puddings which have white of egg piled on top.

SEASONING (STUFFING)

1 small onion
1 cup white breadcrumbs
Pinch herbs
1 tablespoon butter
$\frac{1}{4}$ teaspoon salt
Pinch pepper
1 tablespoon chopped parsley

1. Blanch the onion by putting it in cold water, and bringing to the boil.
2. Drain the water off, put into fresh boiling water, and cook until tender.
3. Drain in a colander.
4. Chop the onion finely and put into a basin.
5. Add all the other ingredients and mix well.

Note. This is used for seasoning ducks, geese, and pork.

TO BLEND FLOUR

2 level tablespoons flour
$\frac{2}{3}$ cup milk or water

1. Put the flour into a small basin.
2. Make a well in the centre and gradually stir in the liquid, using a wooden spoon.
3. Mix till quite smooth.

TO BEAT EGG WHITE

1. Put the egg white on a flat dinner plate and use a dinner knife.
2. Hold the plate quite level, and while beating, keep the knife flat on the plate.
3. Beat quickly, keeping as much of the egg as possible moving over the knife at one time, until quite stiff.

TO CHOP PARSLEY

1. Wash the parsley and dry well.
2. Pick the leaves off the stalks.
3. Gather the parsley up tightly in the fingers and cut it with a sharp knife.
4. Do this several times, then hold the point of the knife downwards on the board and chop with the end nearest the handle till very fine.

INDEX

A

Aberdeen sausage	17
Almond paste icing	115
Anchovy and egg	3
Anchovy sauce	145
Angel's food	66
Anzac biscuits	119
Apple, baked	155
Apple amber pudding, baked	80
Apple and rice meringue	78
Apple cake	101, 103
Apple chutney	146
Apple delight	155
Apple dumplings, baked	95
Apple jelly	149
Apple pie	95
Apple pudding	72, 73
Apple sauce	140
Apple snow	79
Apple sponge	79
Apples, casseroled	85
on sticks	152
stewed	85
Apricot jam	149
Apricot pudding, baked	80
Apricots, stewed	86
stewed dried	86
Arrowroot gruel	156
Artichokes, globe	39
Jerusalem	39
Asparagus	36
Asparagus and ham dip	64

B

Bacon, fried	1
and tomato	1
Bacon and egg, fried	3
Bacon and egg pie	57
Bacon and fried brains	19
Bacon rolls, grilled	18
Banana custard	81
Banana fritters	89
Barley water	156
Basic biscuit recipes	119–120
Basic plain cake	101
Batters	88–90
Bean and onion casserole	51
Beans	37
broad	37
dried, how to cook	51
Beef, cooking uses,	xv
corned	18
cuts of	xv
roast	18, 50
Beef olives	17

Beef tea	156, 157
Beef tea custard	157
Beetroot, boiled	37
cold	45
Biscuit pastry	91
Biscuits and slices	119–127
Blackberry jam	150
Blancmange	67
Boiled rice	5
Boiled icing	115
Boned shoulder of lamb	
or mutton	24
Brain cakes	157
Brains, fricasseed	158
fried, and bacon	19
scalloped	158
Bread and butter custard	68
Bread and milk	159
Bread pudding	159
Bread sauce	140
Breadcrumbs	164
Breads and yeast cookery	133–137
Breakfast cookery	1–5
Broad beans	37
Broccoli	38
Broth, chicken	160
mutton, beef or veal	7
Brown bread	133
Buns, yeast	137
Butter, green (for steak)	165
Butterscotch pie	96
Butterscotch tarts	100

C

Cabbage	38
Cake icings and fillings	115–118
Cakes	101–114
Caper sauce	145
Capsicums, stuffed	51
Caramel	164
Caramel fingers	121
Caramel icing	115
Caramel sauce	141
Carrot and lemon jam	150
Carrots	38
Casserole, apples or pears	85
chicken	55
meat balls	60
rhubarb	87
steak and pineapple	64
vegetable	51
Cauliflower	38
au gratin	52
Celery	39
and spaghetti au gratin	52
Champagne pastry	91

Cheese and vegetable bake	54
Cheese and vegetable pie	54
Cheese balls	52
Cheese biscuits	121
Cheese cakes	104
Cheese custard, baked	53
Cheese dip	63
Cheese loaf or scones	129
Cheese sauce	145
Cheese souffle	53
Cheese souffle tarts	54
Cheese straws	121
Cheeseburgers and mince	60
Cheesecake	97
Cherry and nut drops	121
Cherry and nut ring	131
Cherry cake	103
Cherry creams	153
Chicken, baked	19
fricasseed	25
Chicken and almonds	55
Chicken broth	160
Chicken casserole	55
Chicken cream	56
Chicken mornay	58
Chicken pie	20
Children, dishes suitable for	155–163
Chips, potato	41
Chocolate biscuits	122
Chocolate cake	102
Chocolate coconut slice	122
Chocolate cookies	120
Chocolate eclairs	104
Chocolate fudge fingers	123
Chocolate icing	116
Chocolate pudding	74
Chocolate sauce pudding	81
Choko chutney	146
Chokoes	39
Chops, curried	23
grilled	20
haricot	21
stewed, and rice	160
Choux pastry	91
Christmas cake	104
Christmas pudding	73
Chutney, pickles and	
bottled sauce	146–148
Cinnamon crumble ring	105
Cinnamon drops	123
Clarified fat	164
Clear soup stock	6
Cocoa	1
Coconut cake	102
Coconut chocolate slice	122
Coconut ice	152, 153
Coconut roughs	121
Coconut tarts	100
Cod, smoked	16
Coffee, milk	2
Coffee rolls	132
Cold meat cookery	47–50
Coleslaw	44
College pudding	74
Confectionery and sweets	152–154
Convalescent, dishes	
suitable for	155–163
Cookery terms	xix
Corn, sweet	42
Corn fritters	56
Corned beef	18
Cornflake crisps	123
Cornflour gruel	156
Cornish pasties	21
Cream filling, mock	117
Cream filling for cakes	117
Cream puffs	105
Creamed rice shape	84
Crisp or snap biscuits	127
Crown roast of lamb	26
Crumbed fried cutlets	22
Cup and spoon measurements	x
Currant pudding, steamed	76
Curried chops	23
Curried eggs	57
Curried steak	23
Curry and rice	47
dry	22
egg and lentil	59
Curry sauce	145
Custard, baked	67
baked cheese	53
banana	81
beef tea	157
bread and butter	68
for puffs	106
macaroni	69
puffs	106
rice	69
sago	69
steamed	68, 160
stirred	70
vermicelli	69
Custard puffs	105
Custard sauce	142
Custard tart	97
Cutlets, crumbed fried	22
French	22

D

Date chutney	147
Date drops, spicy	121
Date loaf	132
Date pudding, steamed	76
Date scones	129
"Dribarm" bread	134
Dried apricot jam	149
Dry curry	22
Dumplings, baked apple	95

E

Eclairs, chocolate	104
Egg, fried, and bacon	3
poached	4
scrambled	4
steamed	4
Egg and anchovy	3
Egg and bacon pie	57
Egg and lentil curry	59
Egg and tomato	3
Egg cutlets	2
Egg flip	161
Egg mornay	58
Egg white, to beat	166
Eggless pudding	75
Eggs, cooked in shells	2
curried	57
hard-cooked for salads	45
sweet poached	84

F

Fat, clarified	164
Filleting of fish	11
Fish	11–16
Fish, baked	11
fried	12
grilled	12
scalloped	14
steamed	13
Fish batter	88
Fish cakes	13
Fish kedgeree	57
Fish mornay	58
Fish stock	6
Fish pies	15
Flaky pastry	92
Flour, to blend	166
Fondant, uncooked	153
Forcemeat	165
French cutlets	33
French dressing	46
French jellies	154
Fricassee, brains	219
lamb, chicken or rabbit	25
tripe and onion	34
Fried bacon and tomato	1
Fried egg and bacon	3
Fried fish	12
Fried rice	62
Fried scones (puftaloons)	129
Fritter batter	88
Fritters, banana	89
corn	56
meat	47
Fruit cake	106
Fruit flummery	81
Fruit icing	116
Fruit or ginger slice	124

Fruit salad	82
Fruits, stewed and casseroled	85–87
Fudge fingers, chocolate	123

G

Gem scones	130
Ginger biscuits	124
Gingerbread	107
Ginger creams	153
Ginger pudding	77
Ginger slice	124
Ginger sponge	106
Globe artichokes	39
Golden syrup sauce	142
Golden top pudding	74
Goulash	23
Grapefruit jam	150
Gravy, brown	140
thin brown	25
Green butter for steak	165
Green peas	40
Gruel	161

H

Haddock, Scotch	16
Haricot chops or steak	21
Horse-radish sauce	142

I

Icings and fillings for cakes	115–118
Irish stew	24

J

Jam roll, baked	99
Jam roll, steamed	76
Jam sauce	142
Jams and jellies	149–151
Jellies, French	154
Jelly, milk	162
Jerusalem artichokes	39
Julienne soup	7
Junket	161

K

Kedgeree, fish	57
Kidney and bacon	58
Kiss cakes	107
Kitchen requisites	ix

L

Lamb, boned shoulder of	24
cooking uses	xvi

crown roast of	26
cuts of	xvi
fricasseed	25
roast	25
Leeks	40
Lemon and carrot jam	150
Lemon cheese	117
Lemon cheese tart, quickly made	98
Lemon cheese tarts	100
Lemon cream pie, crumb-crust	98
Lemon drink	162
Lemon filling for cakes	117
Lemon meringue tart	99
Lemon pudding	74, 82
Lemon sago	83
Lemon sauce	143
Lemon sauce pudding	83
Lemon teacake	108
Lentil and egg curry	59
Lentil or pea soup	8
Liver and bacon	26
Loaf and scone mixtures	128–132

M

Macaroni and salmon	62
Macaroni cheese	59
Macaroni custard	69
Marble cake	103
Marmalade	151
Marrow	40
Marshmallow biscuits	124
Marshmallows	154
Masking sauce	144
Mayonnaise	46
Meat, batter for	88
cuts of, and methods of cooking	xv
joints and accompaniments	xiv
timetable for cooking	xiv
Meat and poultry dishes	17–35
Meat balls, casseroled	60
Meat fritters	47
Meat loaf	48
Melted butter sauce	144
Melting moments	125
Meringue shell, economical	108
Meringues	108
Metric conversions	xii
Metric cup and spoon measurements	x
Milk coffee	2
Milk jelly	162
Milk puddings	66–71
Mince, tomato and vegetable	65
Mince and cheeseburgers	60
Mince and spaghetti	64
Mince roll, grilled	26
Mince tart	99

Minestrone	8
Mint sauce	143
Miscellaneous	164–166
Mock cream filling	117, 118
Mulligatawny soup	9
Mustard pickle	147
Mustard sauce	145
Mutton, boned shoulder of	24
cooking uses	xvi
cuts of	xvi
roast	27
simmered	27

N

Nectarines, stewed	86
Nut and cherry ring	131
Nut loaf	132
Nut roast	61
Nutties	125

O

Oats, rolled	5
Omelet, savoury	162
sweet	163
Onion sauce	144
Onions	40
Orange cake	102
Orange filling for cakes	117
Orange icing	116
Orange pudding	74
Ox tongue, simmered	34
Oxtail, stewed	28
Oyster soup	9
Oysters, scalloped	14

P

Panada sauce	200
Pancake batter	89
Pancakes	89
Parsley, to chop	166
Parsley butter	165
Parsley sauce	144
Parsnips, boiled	38
Passionfruit shape	83
Pasties, Cornish	21
Pastry	91–94
sweet	95–100
Patty cakes	103
Pavlova	109
Pea or lentil soup	8
Peanut biscuits	125
Peaches, stewed	86
Pears, casseroled	85
stewed	85
Peas, green	40
Pickle, mustard	147
Pikelets	109

Pink sugar	165	Sago custard	69
Plain cake, basic	101	Sago fruit pudding	75
Plain cakes	110	Salad vegetables, preparation of	43
Plum jam	151	Salads and salad dressings	43–46
Plum pudding, sago	75	Salmon and macaroni	62
Plum sauce	147	Salmon mayonnaise	15
Plums, stewed	86	Salmon souffle	53
Poached egg	4	Sandwich cake, sponge	112
Poached eggs, sweet	84	Sandwiches	138–139
Pork, cooking uses	xvii	Sauces, bottled	147–148
cuts of	xvii	Sauces and gravy	140–145
roast	28	Sausage, Aberdeen	17
sweet and sour	60	Sausage rolls	30
Porridge, wheatmeal	5	Sausages, fried	29
Pot roast	29	Savoury dips	63
Potato cakes and bacon	61	Savoury dishes	51–65
Potato puffs	62	batter for	88
Potatoes	41, 42	Savoury omelet	162
Poultry and meat dishes	17–35	Savoury sauce, economical	143
Prunes, stewed	86	Scalloped fish	14
Puddings, milk	66–71	Scalloped oysters	14
steamed or boiled	72–77	Scalloped potatoes	12
summer	78–84	Scone and loaf mixtures	128–132
Puff pastry	92	Scotch haddock	16
Puftaloons (fried scones)	129	Sea pie	31
Pumped leg, simmered	27	Seasoning	166
Pumpkin, boiled	42	Seed cake	104
Pumpkin scones	131	Sheep's tongues, simmered	34
		Shepherd's pie	49
Q		Shortbread	126
		Shortcrust pastry	93
Queen pudding	71	Smoke cod or haddock	16
Quinces, stewed	87	Snap biscuits	127
		Souffle, cheese	53
R		Souffle tarts, cheese	54
		Soups and stocks	6–10
Rabbit, baked	19	Spaghetti and celery au gratin	52
fricasseed	25	Spaghetti and mince	64
Rabbit pie	20	Spaghetti bolognaise	63
Rainbow cake	110	Spanish cream	66
Raspberry buns	111	Spice cake	103
Raspberry slices	126	Spicy date drops	121
Refrigerator biscuits	126	Spinach	38
Relish, tomato	148	Sponge cake, large	113
Rhubarb, casseroled	87	Sponge sandwich	112
stewed	87	Spoon and cup measurements	x
Rice, baked	71	Squash	40
boiled	5	Steak, curried	23
fried	62	grilled	31
vegetable	65	haricot	21
Rice and apple meringue	78	sharp	31
Rice custard	69	Steak and kidney pie	32
Rice shape	84	Steak and kidney pudding	33
Rissoles	48	Steak and kidney with scone	
Rock cakes	111	topping	33
Rolled oats	5	Steak and pineapple casserole	64
Royal icing	116	Steamed or boiled puddings	72–77
		Steamed fish	13
S		Stew, Irish	24
Sago cream	70	Stocks and soups	6–10

Stock for clear soup	6
Stollen	136
Stuffing	166
Stuffed capsicums	51
Stuffed tomatoes	49
Suet crust	94
Sugar, pink	165
Sultana cake	113
Sultana pudding, steamed	76
Sultana scones	129
Summer puddings	78–84
Swede turnips	42
Sweet and sour pork	60
Sweet corn	42
Sweet poached eggs	84
Sweet sauce	145
Sweet white sauce	145
Sweets and confectionery	152–154
Swiss roll	114

T

Tapioca cream	70
Tarts, butterscotch	100
cheese souffle	54
coconut	100
custard	100
lemon cheese	100
Tea	5
Teacake, lemon	108
Terms used in cookery	xix
Timetable for meat cookery	xiv
Toffee	154
Tomato and bacon, fried	1
Tomato and egg	3
Tomato and vegetable mince	65
Tomato cream soup	10
Tomato jam	151
Tomato relish	148
Tomato sauce	148
Tomatoes, stuffed	49
Tossed salad	44
Treacle sauce	142
Tripe and onion, fricasseed	34
Tuna or salmon with macaroni	90
Turnips, Swede	42
white	42

U

Uncooked coconut ice	153
Uncooked fondant	153
Urney pudding	77

V

Vanilla biscuits	119
Veal, roast	35
Vegetable and cheese bake	54
Vegetable and cheese pie	54

Vegetable and tomato mince	65
Vegetable casserole	51
Vegetable cream soup	10
Vegetable rice	65
Vegetable salad	44
Vegetables	36–42
preparation of, for salad	43
Vermicelli custard	69
Vienna schnitzel	35

W

Warm icing	116
Welsh rarebit	65
Wheatmeal biscuits	127
Wheatmeal porridge	5
White bread	134, 135
White sauce	144

Y

Yorkshire pudding	90
Yeast buns	137

Z

Zucchini	40